LOVING

BIBLICAL PRINCIPLES FOR BUILDING AND
MAINTAINING LOVING RELATIONSHIPS

TIMOTHY RICHMOND

Edited by
JESSICA TANIS

CONTENTS

LOVE DEFINED

Loving

—a Biblical Principles for Developing
a Meaningful Loving Relationships—

Maintaining Bridges

A husband, who had formal Bible training and knew biblical principles well, met with me one day. He was emotionally disturbed and seeking help. He came with his mistress asking for counsel, yet inside he knew that he needed to leave her and return to his wife of five years. His mistress was not a Christian and was very confused.

As we talked about God's Word in their situation, they were faced with a difficult situation. His true wife no longer desired his attention; he had stopped maintaining his relationship with his wife and had started a new bridge/relationship with another woman. After years of disrepair and neglect, how could he return to loving his wife? Had he burnt that bridge forever?

Sharon did well for herself. She made money and lived in comfort in NYC. But when she died it was apparent that she did well *for herself*. She had cut off all her family and lived completely to herself. Her funeral was eerie, attended by just a handful of people. The man who spoke knew nothing about her, and anyone who knew a little about her saw that anything positive the speaker stated about Sharon was the exact opposite of her life.

Many similar stories could be repeated. The world is filled with people who have ruined relationships, and some have ruined every relationship they have entered. Perhaps you have lived through the hurtful side of a family relationship, either as a child or as a spouse. Marriages have hit a low in success rates both inside and outside the church. Families often are destroyed by divorce, and those who survive divorce usually are far from thriving. Relationships in other areas, too, are often strained. Workplace tensions are often extremely difficult to bear because of relationship problems with co-workers.

Why are people so poor at relationships? I propose that this is the case because people don't work at relationships. Married couples do not work to maintain their marriages. People work on their house or apartment; they work on their occupational development; they work on their fitness; they maintain so many facets of their life except this extremely vital one – human relationships. And yet it is never too late to start building and maintaining!

This book is written to help you build stronger relationships. These lessons were developed for pre-marital counseling, so they are designed primarily for spouses or engaged couples; but they can easily be applied to every relationship. Why? Because the majority of the lessons deal with the topic of love, and love is the answer to every relationship problem.

If you follow through with these lessons, I know you will be a stronger spouse. Whether you are beginning these lessons because you are considering marriage, or better yet, you are serious about improving your existent marriage relationship, I want you to be encouraged that marriage is a delightful gift. When maintained properly, it can be God's gift of lifelong, joyful companionship. But it takes work along the way – bridge building work.

Think of your life as an island in the middle of the ocean. Every other individual alive today is a small island surrounding you, some in closer proximity than others. In order to interact with these other islands, you must build bridges. These bridges are relationships. Some bridges were built for you because of where you were born (family, neighborhood, school). Other bridges you seek to build on your own.

At times you may need to break down a bridge because too much hazardous waste comes from one island to your island across that bridge. At other times, you try to build a bridge to a person, and they reject your offer. Some people are better than others at building bridges; some people are better at maintaining bridges. Sad to say, some people are only good at destroying every bridge they see – not just their own!

A large part of your life is managing the trade and commerce back and forth between these bridges. Be careful what you send out and what you take in. Be careful who is building their bridge onto your island. Most importantly, as Christians, we must think of the billions of other islands on the earth as opportunities to bridge the gap and share Christ.

Let's use this illustration to consider our current study. In close relationships, especially in marriage, that bridge is essential. The bridge you built to your spouse was most likely carefully crafted and purposefully planned out. For some, these blueprints would make an architect blush. Once you found that this relationship was special, you made sure the bridge was well paved, sturdy, and that only the best fruit from your island made it to his or her island. You went out of your way to protect that relationship.

In time, this careful treatment and conscientious following of the rules that govern our relationships breaks down. We take for granted the bridge between us. The well-paved path grows bumpy. The time and effort we pour into establishing new bridges at work or in other settings are now missing from this most  important relationship. And the bridge begins to crack. We are no longer careful to repair every pothole, and we allow time to decay the bridge.

When we allow this state of decay, the smallest storm can cause a great rift. And so marriages sour and relationships ruin. This usually happens not because of one major storm, but because a married couple has allowed years to go by without repairing their relationship. They have not put time and effort into understanding how to maintain a loving relationship.

Where do I learn bridge building?

Where should we go to get these types of principles which help us build and maintain strong bridges? I remember listening to a public radio interview with two marriage counselors who gave advice to couples. As the program unfolded, we found that they had been divorced. Although they may give some good advice, I'd like to ask someone who is successful for successful principles in marriage. I've been married for over sixteen years, and although I believe our marriage is wonderful, that hardly gives you a reason to wade through this material – after all, it's only been twenty years.

So, let me tell you up front that the principles presented here are found in the Bible, which is why they are profitable.

In this book, we will discover the Scriptural principles to help build a loving relationship. Although these principles can be applied to just about any relationship, we are going to specifically apply them to marriage: for those who are preparing for marriage or, more importantly, for those who desire a flourishing rather than just a functioning marriage.

Half of the booklet will focus on love as it applies to all relationships in general. Biblical love is the only way to build and maintain the strongest of bridges. It is essential if you want to have a long and prosperous marriage. And yet as I prepared for marriage, I was surprised at the lack of resources available that teach what true love is. However, God does

 share these life-changing truths in His Word, the Bible. As we go through these chapters, you will find them very practical and extremely helpful. They are God's words for us, helping us build and maintain proper loving relationships. As I've used these truths in counseling over the past ten years, I've seen so many eyes open up to the simple and yet profound way God shares how to love one another. You will see that the principles in these chapters also apply to any relationship at church, home, or the office. Try to love as Christ loved. You will see a radical difference in your life.

In chapters five and six we will apply these love principles to two major areas that often need tending on our bridges – forgiveness and communication. The final two chapters will develop God's principles for marriage roles in particular. God designed marriage, so He knows how it works best. Work your way through all the lessons and work hard to complete the questions at the end of the lessons as well.

Whether you have been married for fifty years or want to have God's mind about all relationships, I know the thoughts and principles shared with you in these pages do work. God promises that they can transform your relationships. So let's begin! Let's begin with the key to love.

What is the key to love?

The phrase, "this is the key!" is overused today. At times, it over simplifies a topic with an easy solution. But in the rest of our lesson, we are going to highlight the key to love. And I think you will agree that we are not oversimplifying the topic. This key is found in the Bible.

What is Love?

Before we look at what this key is, we should get an overview of what love is. We will spend the next few lessons developing the Bible's concept of love. This term often is referred to by the Greek verb *agape*. It is what Jesus mirrored for us on the cross by giving everything for us with nothing in return. As we begin the study, let's take a stab at a summary definition: *giving of yourself to serve another individual with no thought for return.* This is the biblical concept of love. Let's contrast this with a few popular misconceptions of love.

Love is not 50/50.

You may have heard that relationships are give and take, 50/50. You give 50% and your spouse gives 50%, and *voila!* you have a working marriage. This is a horrible misconception of love. Love is giving 100% of yourself to your spouse with no thought of return. You may be tempted to give 50% so that they will give 50% back. But that is an improper concept of love. Love is giving 100% of yourself with no thought whatsoever of return from the other person. So, in order for a marriage to work, each person must be giving 100% of himself or herself to the other person.

If two spouses are committed to doing this, you will have a loving marriage relationship. Already you are thinking deep down, "Well, yes, I would if he would chip in at least 25%!" But again, that is where your thinking is incorrect. We cannot work on changing the other until we are consistently giving 100% of ourselves to the marriage. Biblical love gives 100% with no thought of return.[1]

Love is not Lust.

Our culture often equates love with lust. If you listen to the popular message of entertainment media, the world equates a physical urge for sex with love. Our culture highlights "love at first sight" as a romantic ideal. But how can someone truly love someone if they have never met them? Can someone really serve another person with no thought of return by just glancing ("first sight")? Lust is "me-centered"; love is "others-centered." Love is not lust and frankly is often the opposite. Never marry based entirely on looks. Looks change, so if that spouse married you only for looks, then they will leave you when they find attraction elsewhere.

Love is not Obsession.

Often dating couples are so attached that they are obsessed with the other person. We may mistakenly think that the more someone is distracted by the other person, the more they love them. Yet distraction may actually be a selfish control issue. You may think so much about your fiancé or spouse that you are distracted or absent-minded. Your love should be defined by your self-sacrificing service to the other person not in your obsession with them. The feeling of "obsession" may wear off after a while. But love never fails.

Love is not easy.

The phrases "fall in love" and "fall out of love" are misleading. The focus of these phrases is the ease with which you are able to turn on love or turn off love. "It is something I fell into." You may be attracted to another person very quickly by sight or after an initial meeting. You can fall into attraction. But true love, sacrificially serving another with no thought of return, takes time and effort.

> We choose to love no matter what we are
> feeling at the present time

The problem with falling in love is the opposite – falling out of love. It is as if they had no choice. "One night I went to bed loving my spouse, and something happened when I woke up; I had fallen out of love!" It's as if they fell off the bed inadvertently. The conclusion that corresponds to this is that they are giving up on the relationship. "I fell out of love, so I don't have to build this bridge anymore." This view of love is the opposite of Bible love. We never fall out of love. We choose to love when it is easy *and* hard. We choose to love no matter how we feel at the present time.

God is Love.

The Bible says, "God is love" (1 John 4:8). This phrase really teaches the Bible's understanding of love. In fact, the greatest demonstration of this love was when Jesus died on the cross for our sins. This was the greatest gift of sacrifice. You have probably heard the following verses (emphasis added):

> "For *God so loved* the world, *that He gave* His only begotten Son, that whoever believes in Him shall not perish, but have eternal life" (John 3:16).

"But God demonstrates *His own love* toward us, in that while we were yet sinners, Christ died for us" (Romans 5:8).

You see from these two verses that God's love is defined by *God's giving* toward us. He loved us so much that He gave His most prized possession – His Son, Jesus. His giving was with nothing to receive in return. Though we give our lives to Him, He needs nothing. In fact, we did not deserve His love; we deserved His wrath. Think of the following verses:

"For all have sinned and fall short of the glory of God" (Romans 3:23).

"All of us like sheep have gone astray, Each of us has turned to his own way" (Isaiah 53:6).

Would you love someone who resisted you every day, or perhaps every hour of the day? Probably not! And yet this describes every person in the world according to the Bible. God gives us clear commands as parameters to live by. Yet, we reject those commands, insist on going our own way, and stray away from His love. We now sin on a daily basis. None of us deserve God's love.

Because we have broken God's commands, He sent His Son, Jesus, to take the punishment for our law breaking. He was the sacrifice in our place. He was your sacrifice. He took God's wrath for you. What great sacrifice! What great love!

Have you ever come to accept God's gift of love? Have you believed in this good news? Have you trusted in Jesus as the sacrifice for your own sin? This is the true key to loving others. That is what we will examine next.

You Can't Love.

God's love to us demonstrated in Jesus is the standard by which our love is measured. If you want to know true love, then you examine Jesus. He gave all He could to those who were the most unloving. If we take God's love for us through Jesus, we will begin to grasp the essence of love. Let's consider a couple examples of how difficult true love can be.

1. Can you treat someone with kindness when they fly off the handle at you? Let's say you and your husband each have a very difficult day at work. When he comes home, you have spent time already straightening the house and making his favorite meal. However, when you begin to eat, he just mopes. When you ask him about it, he lashes out at you and shouts – "Just leave me alone woman!" How would you respond to this situation?

2. Can you forgive those who mistreat you? A wife who was adjusting to the idea of a marriage went out and spent $25,000 on furniture and other expensive purchases. As a husband, can you forgive your wife and work quietly/sweetly for years together on a strict budget to deal with the debt?

These two situations are very difficult. Some would say they are impossible. And yet, more challenging than these, Jesus actually forgave those who were *putting Him to death*. God actually gave His best gift to those that mistreated Him most. For you, then, you can forgive and love those when God loves through you.

God can love through you.

In his letter to the church in Galatia, Paul describes this dynamic by outlining the difference between the flesh and the Spirit. By flesh he means our natural disposition, our default setting by birth. By Spirit, he means God the Holy

Spirit living through us as believers. Paul begins the contrast between the flesh and the Spirit when commanding to love.

> "But through love serve one another. For the whole Law is fulfilled in one word, in the statement, 'You shall love your neighbor as yourself.' But if you bite and devour one another, take care that you are not consumed by one another" (Galatians 5:13-15).

Paul tells them to love so that they don't mistreat one another. He goes on to explain the dynamic of the difference between the flesh and the Sprit. The way to walk in love is to walk by God's Spirit living through you.

> "But I say, walk by the Spirit, and you will not carry out the desire of the flesh. For the flesh sets its desire against the Spirit, and the Spirit against the flesh; for these are in opposition to one another, so that you may not do the things that you please." (Galatians 5:16-17)

Those who are born again have God's grace living through them. God is able to work His character in their lives. You can live in a way that you were not able to when in your natural strength. Now, let's examine the difference between the works of the flesh and the works of the Spirit.

Fruit of the flesh

"But if you are led by the Spirit, you are not under the Law. Now the deeds of the flesh are evident, which are: immorality, impurity, sensuality, idolatry, sorcery, enmities, strife, jealousy, outbursts of anger, disputes, dissensions, factions, envying, drunkenness, carousing, and things like these, of which I forewarn you, just as I have forewarned you, that those who practice such things will not inherit the kingdom of God" (Galatians 5:18-21). That sounds like a list you might hear in a divorce court. We are all born with these types of activities coming naturally to us. Just as a dog is born chasing squirrels or leaving his mark for other neighborhood dogs, we are born able to cause factions and disputes. But we don't have to act that way. Look next at the fruit that characterizes the Spirit's influence in our lives.

Fruit of the Spirit

"But the fruit of the Spirit is love, joy, peace, patience, kindness, goodness, faithfulness, gentleness, self-control; against such things there is no law. Now those who belong to Christ Jesus have crucified the flesh with its passions and desires. If we live by the Spirit, let us also walk by the Spirit. Let us not become boastful, challenging one another, envying one another" (Galatians 5:22-26).

What I'm saying to start out our studies together is that it is impossible for you to love consistently on your own. But there is hope. God is love, and He can live His love through you! That is the key to the Christian life.

Making God's Love Your Love

You can take on God's love by accepting Jesus as your Lord and Savior. Believe in the Lord Jesus, and you will be saved from a life of "flesh-like" living in marriage. Be empowered today.

Be saved through faith. True saving faith goes deeper than believing in the reality of a historical person named Jesus. It goes beyond believing that this Person is God and that He died on a cross. In fact it goes even deeper than believing that Jesus died for sins. True saving faith believes that Jesus died for *your* sins in particular. Your sins offended the holy, creator God, but that God has paid the penalty for your sins through the death of His Son, Jesus. If you trust this to be true, then you ask Jesus for that forgiveness that is possible through His death on the cross.

You should think of the cross on which Jesus died as God's bridge from heaven to your island. God the Father, through God the Son, reached out to make a relationship with you. He demonstrated His love to you even when you had no interest in Him, even when you were a sinner.[2] When you open your heart to that bridge – when you receive that relationship – you are enabled to live the same love demonstrated by the cross. Saving faith in Jesus is the beginning of a relationship where He resides in you and enables you to live a new spiritual life, a born again life, a loving life. The fruit of God begins to grow in you.

One fruit that God develops in you is love. *This* is the key to a loving relationship. Anyone can love for an hour a week, but God's love must withstand 24/7 exposure to the elements for years on end. This is impossible to do consistently apart from God. In the chapters to come, we will delve much deeper into all the practical aspects of that one fruit of love. But you really cannot move on to perfecting all the nuances of love in your marriage if you have not started with God's love.

Let me encourage you to start by accepting God's love for yourself. If you don't start there, then all the other things will be helpful advice only, knowledge without power. This first lesson is foundational because it gives the impetus, the engine, to love. The practical details can be developed and fine-tuned through years of experience and practice. But the engine must be Christ and His Spirit, or you will always end up frustrated.

Chapter 1 Homework

1. Contrast the fruit of the flesh with the fruit of God's Spirit.

Fruit of the Spirit (Galatians 5:18-21)	Fruit of the Flesh (Galatians 5:22-26)
Sexual immorality	love
impurity	joy
Sensuality	peace
idolatry	patience
sorcery	Kindness
enmity	goodness
strife	faithfulness
jealousy	gentleness
anger	self control
envy	

2. Have you ever trusted in Jesus as your Savior from sin? When did you ask Jesus for His forgiveness and commit your life to Him?

3. How have you seen God developing in you the character traits listed on the second column above?

4. What parts of the first column do you see as the most challenging in your relationships? Which part of the second column do you see as the most helpful for a marriage relationship?

LOVE DESCRIBED PART 1

Loving

Biblical Principles For Developing
& Maintaining Loving Relationships

I
f we all loved perfectly, all of the world's problems would be erased. This is not an exaggeration. Jesus summarized the moral requirements of the entire Bible in one word: love. The world would be a utopia if we could just keep that one commandment. So when we consider relationships, we must take time to understand what love is; this understanding is essential. No doubt if this is essential, God would describe this vital activity to us in detail. And He has – in what is commonly called "the love chapter."

In chapters 2-4, we will follow the activities of love outlined in 1 Corinthians 13. If we were to outline the entire chapter, we could divide it into three sections.

- The essential nature of love (vv. 1-3)
- The active nature of love (vv. 4-7)
- The eternal nature of love (vv. 8-13)

The description of love is found in that second section,

love's active nature, so we will focus carefully on that section. Let's walk through verses 4-7:

> "Love is patient, love is kind and is not jealous; love does not brag and is not arrogant, does not act unbecomingly; it does not seek its own, is not provoked, does not take into account a wrong suffered, does not rejoice in unrighteousness, but rejoices with the truth; bears all things, believes all things, hopes all things, endures all things. Love never fails" (1 Corinthians 13:4-8).

These verses can be divided into three separate sections:

- Love's essential activities
- Love's "not" activities
- Love's all-encompassing activities

You will notice that each of these categories involves action[1]. You cannot love if you do not have action. Remember in our first lesson we defined love as "giving of yourself." Giving of yourself is active. If you are not giving of yourself, then you are not loving.

Let's begin with love's essential activities. These are two actions that make the rest work and summarize the other activities to follow. You could really hang all of them onto one of either of the first two activities. So be prepared to get these two down well. We will call them love's essential activities.

Love's Essential Activities

What a great one-two punch the first two activities of love make! The equation is simple – Love is patient, love is kind.

1. Love is patient.

Let's start with patience. What is patience? The root word is a combination word coming from the word "long" and the word "anger." The idea is that it takes a long time before the person is angry.

Imagine you put a pot of water on the stove. You turn on the gas and wait for it to boil. If it took the pot a few minutes to boil, you would say it was unusual. Well, what if it took all day and all night to boil – and the burner is on high! That would be our word patient. It takes a long time before it boils. That is love. Love is not immediately annoyed. It waits and waits before it boils.

This is essential in any relationship, but especially in a marriage. You are together every day. The pleasantries wear off quickly. Love is patient. We could put it another way. If you are not patient with your spouse, then you are not loving. You can say you love them all you want, but if you fly off the handle (boil) at the slightest problem, then you are not loving. Love goes deeper than words to actions.

Some people are more difficult to love just because of their personal idiosyncrasies. They may have an odd sense of humor or quirky habits. Spouses can have odd hobbies like collecting suitcases or playing loud instruments, so if your spouse does not have anything like this, be thankful! If they do, continue to be patient. You have some of these too.

More likely, you will need to learn to be patient with the small things in life that tend to irritate us. Things like refilling the toilet paper roll in the bathroom or squeezing the toothpaste tube from the bottom to top (as anyone knows that is the only correct way to brush your teeth) can set us off. If we are honest, these become the difficult things in marriage. And if you allow these things to "snowball" without being truly patient on the inside, you damage your marriage relationship.

What area do you need exceptional patience? Please take time to communicate with your spouse about areas that they are easily impatient with you. As you communicate about these areas, you are more ready to love your spouse by being patient with them.

Patience is essential in a church setting because we all have different backgrounds, expectations, and personalities. We are all different members by design, so we will need to have great patience with others in our church. Do you over-react to the small miscommunications or inadvertent inconveniences that arise from a fellow church attender? Do you react at all to these small things? If you react to their actions for your own well-being, then you are not a loving member at your church. You are selfish, and a selfish church member is either controlled by their flesh rather than God's Spirit, or they are unsaved. A loving member will want to help, but it does not boil for its own sake.

2. Love is kind.

The next activity also is found in verse 4. "Love is kind." This is the opposite side of the coin of patience. As you are being patient, you are not retaliating to unkindness with anger. It is not enough just to be passive in receiving difficulty from a spouse. Beyond this, you must respond actively in kindness. Not only do you not retaliate negatively, in anger; you retaliate positively, in kindness. Now that is love!

Kindness is treating one another in the way you would like to be treated: "The Golden Rule." In order to get a better picture of what this word means, consider how Jesus uses the word in Matthew 11:30. He says that His yoke and burden are "easy" or light to carry. This is our word "kind." Being kind is being easy to live with or in a sense, easy to carry. You know people that are difficult to carry. They are just a burden to be around for one reason or another. Perhaps we feel like we are walking on eggshells around them, or their personality is abrasive or difficult to manage. This is the opposite of kindness.

What does kindness look like in a marriage? Kindness smiles, encourages, helps, and listens. Kindness considers the other person's interests and desires first in a decision. These activities are not optional, nor are they activities we can stop once we are married for a long time. We are commanded to treat everyone with kindness in the Bible; this is even so much more the case within a marriage.

"Love is patient, love is kind" – We have identified these first two activities as love's essential activities. If you get this, you get the essence of love. They summarize all of love. You are patient toward those mistreating you, and you are kind to them in return. You can see how this dynamic works in the diagram below and how each of the following activities is really the outworking of these two qualities.

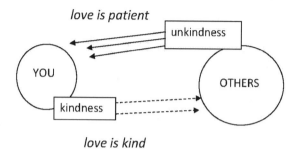

love is patient

love is kind

Love's "Not" Activities

The next section of activities is love's not activities. Notice the next several activities in 1 Corinthians 13:4-6. Each of the next eight activities states what love does not do. When trying to understand something, it is helpful to recognize what that something is not. That is exactly what God does in the next eight facets of love. As you read through the verses below, circle each "not."

> "Love is patient, love is kind and is not jealous; love does not brag and is not arrogant, does not act unbecomingly; it does not seek its own, is not provoked, does not take into account a wrong suffered, does not rejoice in unrighteousness, but rejoices with the truth; bears all things, believes all things, hopes all things, endures all things. Love never fails."

What you do *not* do is just as important as what you *do* in your relationships. Perhaps there are things you must cut out to be truly loving. Let's look at what the Lord states should *not* be a part of any loving relationship.

3. Love is not jealous.

Jealousy can be a positive emotion in a relationship. Marriage is a covenant commitment for life, so it is expected that a spouse will be faithful. In that sense, jealousy can be a positive insistence that a spouse stay faithful to this commitment. God tells us that He is jealous for His people. God wants our undivided love and attention.

However, at times jealousy demonstrates a lack of trust in your spouse. An over-possessive tendency can be a signal of a deeper issue. Perhaps your attachment to your spouse is built entirely on selfishness. When your spouse has any alone time or away time you pressure them or make them feel guilty. This is not healthy in a relationship.

In this verse, Paul is referring to someone who is jealous of the positive things that happen to another. Someone gets jealous when someone else succeeds. You would think that this type of jealousy would never enter a marriage relationship and therefore would not need to be mentioned in a book like this. But it occurs more often than you think.

Some parents are jealous of their children's attention. When a spouse goes through a bad stretch with that child, the other spouse can feel smug or receive some satisfaction that they have a better relationship with that child. This is jealousy. Or, perhaps one spouse receives more attention in public because of their gifts or personality. The loving spouse is not jealous, but rejoices at their husband or wife's accomplishments and does not resent their success one bit.

A church member is not resentful or envious of another

member's gifts or usefulness. When we hear of positive news in the life of another person in our spiritual family, we rejoice with them. Jonathan Edwards defined this non-activity as "a spirit of dissatisfaction with and opposition to the prosperity and happiness of others as compared with our own."[2] This is inconsistent with biblical love. You do not love someone if you are jealous of their success.

4. Love does not brag.

You may never have thought that bragging is a characteristic of an unloving person, but this is clearly true from this passage. You see, bragging is entirely focused on self. It uses words to point to the positive aspects or accomplishments of one's self. This is not love; remember that love is the opposite of selfishness. Remember our beginning definition in the first lesson: "Love is giving of yourself to serve another individual with no thought for return." You can see how a boasting person is the opposite of a loving person.

Instead, a loving person uses their mouth to build up their spouse. One good habit to develop is to speak kindly about your spouse at least once a day. Simple, right? Yes, but it is profound. If we are not careful, we can take for granted that our spouse knows what we think instead of speaking kindly to them. Build up your spouse with your words every day in the next two weeks; you will be truly loving him or her. Also, be specific. Don't just say, "I love you" (hopefully you are already saying that more than once a day). Think of one specific aspect of your spouse that you love and share it with them.

"I like that outfit." "You are so funny!" "I think you are

getting better and better at _____ the longer I know you." "I don't know how your employer could do without you." "You are so beautiful!" "I really enjoy seeing you smile."

Use your imagination. Don't build yourself up – that is unloving. Instead, build up your spouse. This is healthy in every relationship. Use your words to build up others rather than tearing down.

5. Love is not arrogant.

Love does not brag for a very good reason. It does not think much of itself which is love's third "not." It is not arrogant. The word here is literally, "blown up." Love is not puffed up. It does not have a big head.

It is a rather comical word-play. If a person has so many big ideas about himself, his head swells up. You could picture a person that spiritually walks around like a bobble-head doll and has a difficult time getting through the door. His estimation of himself is too high! That is arrogance, and it is not love.

You will find quickly in a relationship how much a person thinks of himself. Nothing in a relationship is as ugly as a person with arrogance. In fact, it is not just ugly; it is something that God hates! If you were to list seven things that God hates, you might list many things that do not fall on the list of seven that the Proverbs gives us. Interestingly, the first one that Solomon mentions is a haughty look. Pride is not just harmful to Christian relationships; it is an abomination in the eyes of God. And it hinders grace in your life. "God resists the proud and gives grace to the humble" (1 Peter 5:5).

Paul has often had to deal with arrogance in the Corinthian church. The word is used more in this book than any other book in the New Testament. They were proud of their associations (4:6, 18-19). They were proud of their tolerance of sin (5:2). They were proud of their knowledge (8:1). They were proud of their gifts (12:31; 13:4). Paul had to emphasize love in such a proud church. Pride is the Achilles' heel of love. If you are proud, you are self-focused and not a loving person. And if you are a proud person then you will negatively affect your church or marriage.

R. A. Torrey shared how the Lord used D. L. Moody so much more because of his humility.

"He was used so much by the Lord as an international evangelist but thought nothing of his own gifts and all of his great God. God continuously, through so many years, used D. L. Moody... because he was a humble man. I think D. L. Moody was the humblest man I ever knew in all my life. He loved to quote the words of another; 'Faith gets the most; love works the most; but humility keeps the most.' He himself had the humility that keeps everything it gets."[3]

Torrey goes on and shares the dangers of pride in any Christian ministry:

"When the Devil cannot discourage a man, he approaches him on another tack, which he knows is far worse in its results; he puffs him up by whispering in his ear: 'You are the leading evangelist of the day. You are the man who will sweep everything before you. You are the coming man. You are the D. L. Moody of the day'; and if you listen to him, he will ruin you. The entire shore of the history of Christian workers is strewn with the wrecks of gallant vessels that were full of promise a few years ago, but these men became puffed up and were driven on the rocks by the wild winds of their own raging self-esteem."[4]

Pride is dangerous. It is poison to any relationship, including marriage.

We need to make one clarification before moving on. This does not mean that we think *poorly* of ourselves. Instead, we think *Scripturally* of ourselves. We realize that all we are or ever will be is because of God's abundant grace. "Not that we are adequate in ourselves to consider anything as coming from ourselves, but our adequacy is from God" (2 Corinthians 3:5). We think much of our God, so we attempt much for His glory and by His grace.

Some who focus on their own weaknesses, sins, and faults too much are still self-focused. Humility is not thinking ill of ourselves; it is thinking so much of God and others that it does not think about itself at all. There is a big difference. You could think poorly about yourself so much that this too is pride. A good example would be Uriah Heep, from Charles Dickens' *David Copperfield*, who so focused on his humility that he sickened others.[5]

Perhaps you have heard how William Carey exemplified this aspect of love. Carey is considered the father of modern missions. He was also a botanist, translator, preacher, and factory manager during his 40-year missionary stay in India. He was very well known in his day, and after his death over 50 biographies have been written about him.

It is evident that love drove his work. He was the opposite of boastful. One time he was invited to a dinner party at a governor's house in India. Many dignitaries were there at this occasion. Carey began in what was considered a low occupation; he mended shoes. One of the guests at the party looked down on Carey because of these "humble beginnings." He asked one of the servants loud enough that others could hear, "I've heard this Carey was once a shoe maker." Carey was not embarrassed; instead, he corrected the man. "No, not even a shoe maker, sir; just a cobbler."

This is the spirit of a loving person. They are not concerned about what others think of them or jealous of others people's attention. They naturally want to build others up. This is possible only through a new nature – the nature of Christ. This is the way Jesus came to us on earth:

> "Have this attitude in yourselves which was also in Christ Jesus, Who, although He existed in the form of God, did not regard equality with God a thing to be grasped, but emptied Himself, taking the form of a bond-servant, and being made in the likeness of men." (Philippians 2:5-7)

Chapter 2 Homework

1. Describe how patience and kindness work together to create a truly loving person.

2. Out of the first five activities and non-activities of love, which do you find yourself most needing of

development? How can a person practically develop in these specific character qualities?

3. Spouses, consider stopping now and taking inventory together with the first five actions of love in the exercise in the appendix.

LOVE DESCRIBED PART 2

Loving

Biblical Principles for Developing
& Maintaining Loving Relationships

The first two activities in this catalog of I Corinthians 13 really get to the essence of love. They define and are the overarching pegs on which all others could be placed. "Love is patient; love is kind." We examined these in the last chapter and began looking at the first three of the "nots" of love. There are certain activities that love does not do. Love does not boast, is not arrogant, and is not jealous. Let's pick up where we left off, learning the other activities that love does not do:

> "[Love] does not act unbecomingly; it does not seek its own, is not provoked, does not take into account a wrong suffered, does not rejoice in unrighteousness, but rejoices with the truth." (I Corinthians 13:5-6)

6. Love does not act unbecomingly.

Most versions translate the word "act unbecomingly" as rude. Love is not rude. It behaves with manners. It behaves properly in the normal cultural sense. Love is not rude in public. It behaves as the cultural norm dictates. It is not out of order. It does things with propriety and good taste. Of course, some components of what is rude vary from culture to culture. In some cultures, it is acceptable to spit on the ground, while others find the practice offensive. Each culture has norms that are expected of a respectful individual. Love does not try to buck the system of cultural norms. It keeps these boundaries.

Paul uses the opposite of this word to describe what is proper in a worship setting. In public worship in a church, all things should be done properly and in order (orderly or "becomingly" 14:40). If this is true in the church worship service, it is certainly the case in your other relationships.

To show love toward our spouse, we must put off rude speech or manners that are inappropriate.[1] Perhaps men struggle with this more than women, but both need to keep their spouse in mind in this regard. Are you considerate in the way you treat your spouse, or are you rude? Love says excuse me. Love says please and thank you. Love is careful how it leaves the bathroom.

Love understands the different manners and etiquette used by the family of the spouse. Men, have you ever asked your wife what manners she would like you to develop  when eating together? Have you learned her family's customs and habits as she grew up? That is probably what she expects from you. Now, if she was the only girl in a family with four brothers, you probably outshine them by far. However, if she is the only child or has two sisters, you really have to work on this one. Love is willing to do that.

7. Love does not seek its own.

Let's move to our next convicting activity of love, perhaps one of the most difficult activities. It really gets to the heart of the matter. Love's activities are not self-seeking. This word is translated in different ways:

"It does not insist on its own way."

"It is not self-seeking."

"It does not demand its own way."

 Literally, love does not seek its own things. You get a good picture of this when you see someone lose their glasses, or perhaps their phone before an important call. They go from this room to that room turning things over, trying to find their beloved object! And you feel sorry for them, so you start seeking with them. Help them seek their own things.

Take that picture and translate that into the way some people live all the time. For them, it is not just a short period of time when they are like that. Their whole life is composed of their head down to the ground seeking their own things. They go from one thing to the next seeking this thing of their own and that thing of their own. To them, you are not really a person, but another thing that happens to help them seek their own things. If you don't help them seek their "own things," then you get run over.

The truth is, we are programmed to try to seek our own welfare, "our own things." So we all are tempted to live like this. We are tempted to see only our own concerns and our own desires. We are tempted to ignore our spouse's wishes, desires, and goals. But a loving spouse sees their spouse's desires and goals as their own. A loving spouse's life is so intertwined that they see the same goals together. "We are one flesh, so what you are seeking I am seeking." We are not two people looking for a lost pair of glasses; we are two eyes looking together for the same pair of glasses.

This was convicting for me when reading through *The Complete Husband* by Lou Priolo.[2] He encourages husbands to know the goals and aspirations of their wives and try their best to contribute to those goals. Let's try to communicate openly about our goals together ("our things") and even those goals that don't immediately involve our family or work obligations.

8. Love is not provoked.

Our next "not" to gnaw on is that love is not provoked. In the root of this word "provoked" is the word "sharp." Love is not easily sharpened or irritated. When I consider this word, I  picture a porcupine whose quills prick up when irritated or a cat whose claws emerge when instigated.

We must not let our culture dictate what is proper in our relationships

It is amazing how quickly people lose their cool and are irritated in NYC. I have seen people at McDonald's or at the library get so irritated that it is really embarrassing. How can they react like this? How can they yell profanities and threaten someone's life just because someone inadvertently stepped in front of them in line? Or even if they did it on purpose, that is no excuse for this type of a sharp outburst! Getting sharp so quickly is the way to die early due to undue stress.

We cannot allow our culture to condition us toward what is proper in our relationships. You cannot get irritated at small things in a marriage. As is often said, "Don't sweat the small stuff." That is good advice. If you are not careful, as you grow old together, you will begin to vocalize your opinion about more things than you need to. Perhaps your spouse's driving abilities need to improve, but complaining about every small detail will not help things out at all. In fact, it probably makes things even worse. Don't allow yourself to get provoked easily.

As you continue your relationship together, you will see that this is really one of the major "not" abilities to master as a husband and wife. Usually spouses are kept from "soaring" in their marriage because they are "souring" in their marriage over small or minor irritations. Consider some helpful hints in dealing with irritations:

Pick your Battles.

You have heard this before. It is good advice. Even now, stop and think of how many things you have picked at today with your husband or wife? Have there been any? Have there been many? If you are someone who is constantly picking and prodding about this and that issue, then you are a person who is too easily pricked. Your claws come out too early. You are too easily irritated.

If this is you, then stop and take note. Allow yourself one thing that you want to see changed (unless something major comes up), and try to stay silent about everything else. You will see a dramatic difference in your spouse if you pick your battles. Which brings me to my second point.

Don't Battle in your Battles.

What happens when you put up with something, and by God's grace you have kept quiet, but feel like it would be best to bring it up to your spouse? Then bring it up in a constructive and kind way. There are two ways to deal with irritations: "Honey, that sweater is not fit for a dog – it makes you look like a murderer or a psycho." Or, "Honey, I bought you a new sweater, what do you think!?" You can see the great difference. I am amazed at how well my wife does this with me. She rarely picks on things to be sharp about and when she does, she is very careful and sweet about them.

However, our natural response is to battle in the battles. Often incendiary language will creep into these harmless situations. Yes, even in the most harmless situation! All of a sudden hand grenades and flamethrowers are being used as we discuss a new salt and pepper shaker or where the salt is stored. It would be silly in any dating couple, but, sad to say, it is too common in married couples.

How quickly do you fly off the handle when reacting to your friends, colleagues, or family members? When you must correct something, are you gracious in how you say what you say as well as what you say? Use these rules that we will expound on more in the chapter on communication:

- Choose the right words (don't use over-exaggerated, universal phrases like "You always..." "You never..." "I hate it when you...")

- Choose the right tone (nonverbal communication speaks louder than words).
- Choose the right time (when both parties are calm and able to focus, as in not immediately after your spouse comes home from work).
- Choose the right place (not in public). There may be times when you take another person to help clarify and communicate with that friend, but most minor issues can be handled when alone.

9. Love does not take into account a wrong suffered.

Our next "not" is an accounting term. "Take into account" has reference to cataloging numbers in a ledger to keep for a record. What this verse is saying is that love does not keep a tidy Excel spreadsheet of all the wrongs suffered by another person. Wrongs suffered just slip out of our minds when love is involved.

This is another major issue in family and other interpersonal relationships. Love does not have an unforgiving spirit. It is a very poor accountant. If you showed up as an accountant and told your employer, "I just don't know where those thousands of dollars went!" You would get fired. That is not good for an accountant, but it is splendid in a marriage relationship. "I realize that my spouse has mistreated me in many ways; I'm sure he has, but I just can't remember any of them. I just forgot to take note of them." This terrible accounting can maintain a wonderful marriage.

This happens often to me as a dad. Once I was wrestling with one of my daughters (at the time she was probably five), and she looked me straight in the eyes and plugged her nose and said, "Daddy, remind me to plug my nose the next time I wrestle with you because your breath stinks." I remember another daughter concentrating with furrowed

brow, looking at me about five inches from my face, and then with a matter-of-factness that really surprised me said, "Daddy, you look like a donkey." Well, those were not very nice things to say, but honestly, I wasn't hurt one bit (although I guess I'm cataloging it in this chapter). I don't care because I love them. Love does not allow something to sour them. It releases the other person. The loving thing to do in most cases is just to forget it.

We will spend an entire lesson in the future dealing with the issue of forgiveness because it is such an important matter in close relationships. For now, let's leave that there and move on to the tenth action of love.

10. Rejoices not in iniquity,

Rejoicing in iniquity is delighting in someone's downfall. It wants to hear negative things about others. Most of the popular culture magazines prey on our desire for this. Why don't we celebrate someone's 40th wedding anniversary in tabloids at the grocery store? Why not highlight the positives in our culture? Because people rejoice in iniquity.

"Did you hear what she did last week?!" "Can you believe he actually..." Love does not do this. Love does not get any pleasure in cutting others down. If you love someone, then you will weep with them when they weep. You will not rejoice when you hear of their failures. You should be your spouse's best cheerleader. You are always in their corner rejoicing in their successes and weeping at their failures.

but rejoices in the truth

The words *truth* and *iniquity* contrast what love celebrates. They both begin with the Greek letter *a*, so Paul is using a literary device. By truth he is most likely contrasting evil or bad events in life. Love does not rejoice in badness, but instead, love rejoices in truth or goodness. Love will celebrate when the spouse has good times and weep in the bad times. This is truly loving.

Chapter 3 Homework

1. Explain how being rude is actually a form of selfishness and not of love.

2. What are some practical ways to "seek another's things" in your church relationships?

3. Jimbob brags about how consistently loving he is. He is most likely not a loving person after all (True/False).

4. Listening to juicy gossip is extremely unloving (True / False).

5. Match the activity of love needed or demonstrated with each situation:

Character trait of love:	Situation to apply:
A. Love is patient. B. Love is kind. C. Love is not jealous. D. Love does not brag. E. Love does not act unbecomingly. F. Love is not self-seeking. G. Love is not provoked. H. Love does not take wrong into account. I. Love does not rejoice in iniquity but rejoices in the truth.	1. Jimbob has forgotten "what's his name's" name the past three times he came to church. What aspect of love should "what's his name" exhibit toward Jimbob? _____
	2. A missionary finds that it is rude to extend their left hand to another person, so they are sure to adapt to the cultural norm. What activity of love is the missionary exhibiting? _____
	3. A teenager spends hours caring for the new baby in the household to give their parents a break.
	4. A co-worker points out how useless your great idea will be once they upgrade the computer system in a couple months. What activity of love must you display in this situation? _____
	5. Jimbob can't stop talking about his creative genius. _____

LOVE DESCRIBED PART 3

Loving

<small>Biblical Principles for Developing
& Maintaining Loving Relationships</small>

W e have examined the first ten activities involved in love. This finishes our survey of the "nots" in the definition of love. Verses 5-6 give us a good idea of what love does not do, and the ways we should not act toward one another if we love. You can say you love your spouse, but if your actions do not add up, your profession of love is false. You do not love a person to whom you are constantly rude. You do not love a person whom you do not forgive. You may say you are a loving church member or family member, but does your claim measure up to God's standard of love?

- Love is patient.
- Love is kind.
- Love is not jealous.
- Love does not brag.
- Is not arrogant.
- Love does not act unbecomingly.
- Love does not seek its own.
- Love is not provoked.

- Love does not take into account a wrong suffered.
- Love does not rejoice in unrighteousness but rejoices in the truth.

Now Paul shifts from the "nots" of love to the "alls" of love. We could define this section as the all-encompassing activities of love. There are certain actions that must be all encompassing in a loving relationship, without exceptions. These are the final five activities of love concluding the list.

> "[Love] bears all things, believes all things, hopes all things, endures all things. Love never fails" (1 Corinthians 13:7-8).

Love's All-Encompassing Activities

11. Love Bears All Things.

This phrase gives an interesting word picture. The word literally means to cover over in order to protect or preserve something. Love covers in order to protect and preserve like an  umbrella protects from rain. There are a few prominent ways this is encouraged in love.

Love Protects from Harm

When you love someone you will want to protect them from evil. As a boy growing up, I used to collect baseball cards with my brothers. We spent most of our money investing in our favorite players' cards. One good lesson we learned in this practice was the value of preserving and protecting what we bought. One of my brothers has not been able to live down the fact that he wrote his name on the back of his most valuable cards so that they would not be stolen. I can still picture his hardly legible handwritten signature scribbled on the back of Darryl Strawberry's rookie card. As we grew older, we learned how to protect the most valuable cards. Other cards were pushed aside and never seen again. This demonstrates what we naturally do with things we value and love. We protect them.

The same is true in a marriage. The way we protect our loved one from difficulties and pressures demonstrates the degree to which we value them. If you love your spouse, you will protect him or her. How can this protection be defined practically?

Protect from Physical Harm

The first aspect of protection is the most evident. A person who loves their spouse will never harm them physically. On the contrary, they will be concerned for their physical well-being. They will try to protect them from being exposed to things that will harm them physically. This is one way that husbands usually show initiative. They often make sure that the house is locked and secure each night. If there is an unusual noise in the other room, he will often inspect the possible intruder. Perhaps wives express this aspect of love when appealing to husbands to eat well or take other health precautions. I've had many people very close to me who either died or suffered great physical harm because they did not listen to the pleading of a loving spouse to change one aspect or another of their physical habits.

Protect from Emotional Harm

In marriage relationships there are more often emotional harms from which we should be careful to protect our spouse. There is more to any person than their physical makeup. We are composed of feelings and emotions, and these need as much protection as our physical bodies. Unfortunately, harming a spouse's feelings becomes a common practice in a marriage. This is extremely detrimental.

Be careful to understand your spouse in this regard. Learn what hurts their feelings. Consider the following practical considerations:

- Don't say negative things about your spouse in public. Always affirm them in front of others.
- Don't speak in harsh tones.
- Be considerate of your spouse's concerns and interests. If he or she loves a certain food, family member, or sports team, try to learn about that interest instead of taking cheap shots at that entity.

Communicate about your feelings. If your spouse does something that hurts your feelings, you have to be open about that so they know how something makes you feel.

Under this thought it is important to summarize what Peter instructs to husbands:

"You husbands in the same way, live with *your wives* in an

understanding way, as with someone weaker, since she is a woman; and show her honor as a fellow heir of the grace of life, so that your prayers will not be hindered" (1 Peter 3:7).

We will study the different roles of a husband and wife in another lesson. This verse is one of the major ones that the Holy Spirit addresses to husbands, instructing them to live with their wives in an understanding way. In this context, Peter commands that the husband must treat his wife as if she is weaker. We realize that Peter is not saying that the wife is unequal. Husbands, we must honor our wives, not take advantage of them.

An appropriate illustration would be a beautiful Tiffany lamp. We might put a beautiful lamp out of reach of a child's grimy grasp. We honor that lamp by treating it with care and admiring the beauty. This is how we are to view our wives. The husband should take her and set her as far from harm as possible. He should be careful how he treats her. She is not a football to be thrown around but a beautiful vessel to be honored and adored.

A valued vessel is protected by placing it out of reach of clumsy hands.

Protect from Spiritual Harm.

Secular counseling may stop here, but this final phase is most important. In order for a marriage relationship to excel, each spouse must be sensitive to God and growing spiritually. We learned this in our first lesson together. You cannot be a good spouse without being unselfish, and you cannot be truly unselfish consistently without God's grace enabling you. It may work for a week or two, but permanent marriages are founded on a continual love that is enabled by a healthy relationship with God. So it is important for you to grow in your spiritual relationship with God.

The following common paradigm can help you understand the concept. As you and your spouse grow spiritually closer to our Creator, you will also grow closer together.

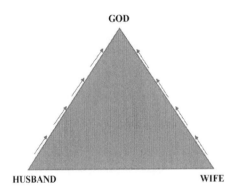

As each person draws closer to God they will also draw closer to their spouse. The reason is that the closer you draw to God, the more you become like Him; as a result, the more you are like Him, the easier you are to live with.

Love Covers Faults

The other way in which love bears or covers is in covering faults. Not only do you cover your spouse with protection (emotionally, physically, and spiritually), but also you strive to cover his or her faults with grace instead of intensifying and dwelling on them. As Peter says, "Above all, keep fervent in your love for one another, because love covers a multitude of sins" (1 Peter 4:8).

A spouse should not use faults as leverage but overlook and cover them from others' view. We don't look with a microscope at our spouse but with a squinting eye so as not to see the faults clearly. This does not mean that we over-look areas that our spouse needs to change to help them improve as a person. But as we considered in an earlier lesson, this means we should be patient with their faults and ask God to help them change.

If a spouse opens up to you about a fault or problem, be careful how you respond. Don't lash out at them but encourage and help them to grow past that fault or problem. You are their number one fan, not their number one critic.

A buried axe should not be used in future battles. Once you have forgiven your spouse for something, don't dwell on that event. Put it out of your memory as much as possible. In some cases, this may take time and include some practical stipulations; however, forgiveness does not keep the forgiven captive. They are released (see chapter 6).

12. Love Believes All Things.

"Love believes all things." Do you trust your spouse? I have seen this matter of trust ruin relationships. Either a spouse betrays a trust or a spouse constantly displays no trust. If you love your spouse, you will trust them. In one sense, this refers to believing in them. "I believe in you, honey!" This attitude of affirmation should be present in every rela-tionship.

But it must go beyond that. A person should also believe

their spouse. When your husband or wife gives you the reason that they were late or were not able to make it to an appointment, love agrees and believes it. It is a bit naive in this way. "Of course my spouse loves me and wants my best. I am going to trust them and believe what they have told me."

A constant debate and challenge over the truthfulness of a claim is harmful. When a spouse constantly checks up and spies on their husband or wife, they are treating them like they do not love them. In the past, when I have met with a husband for personal discipleship, he asked me to send him an email highlighting what we spoke about so that his wife knew that he was actually doing what he said. She would not believe where he was or what he was doing. This was conditioned by a previous relationship she had experienced. However, it was not loving; it was an act of selfish suspicion.

What if your spouse betrays your trust?

Sad to say, a spouse often betrays the trust given by a loving husband or wife. Sexual immorality is not the only place trust is destroyed, but often it is an area where trust is destroyed completely. If a person is unfaithful morally or in a lesser area, that does not mean that the relationship is ruined. A person is able to rebuild trust by faithfulness over an extended period of time. While the spouse is building this trust back, it is not unloving for an increased amount of accountability and oversight. A person may forgive their spouse and still ask for a greater amount of accountability. This is a part of their protection and not their lack of faith in the spouse.

One other concept of believing includes believing God.

Your spouse may have a habit that seems impossible to break. Circumstances may say that he or she will never change in a certain area. Yet, God promises that He can change any person: "With God all things are possible" (Matt. 19:26). He has transformed persecutors (Paul) and prostitutes (Rahab), restored tempers (John, a "son of thunder," became the apostle of love), and broken the hearts of adulterous murderers (David). He can change your spouse, so believe in *Him*!

13. Love Hopes All Things.

This is closely related to the previous "all-inclusive activity" of love. Love hopes for the best of the situation. When love considers the current situation or status of the relationship, it always sees the best days ahead. The glass is half full and with a bit of work it can improve to be much better still.

I remember having a boss who expressed an extremely negative attitude about everything. It was difficult to talk with him. As a Mets fan he was always despondent. If I spoke about the Mets' winning streak, he would say pessimistically that it would not last. Even positive things were turned upside down. This is the way some people live. They have a hard time hoping for the best. A loving spouse knows that they can be a better husband or wife and that the relationship can get even better.

14. Love Endures All Things.

"Love endures all things." The two words that make up the original Greek word are *under* and *remain*. So, the idea behind the word is to remain under. I think of a weight lifter who hefts a large amount of iron above his head and then holds it there. His strength is shown by being able to remain under the weight for a long period of time.

Bear with Your Spouse

Love is able to remain under a large amount of pressure. That is a good thing because marriage brings much pressure. Love does not just endure a little amount of pressure. Love bears up under all things. When you entered the marriage relationship with your spouse, you covenanted to remain under all things with them. At that time you did not know all the pressures you would face as a couple, but now you know some. Remain under all things. When you remain under pressure together you are able to forge your lives together into a beautiful diamond.

This means you may need to bear with habits or idiosyncrasies that you would prefer to avoid. You may have to bear with a spouse's debt. You may have to bear up under your spouse's wrong decisions for a long period of time. The amount of pressure does not afford you the option of leaving. Your covenant is for life.

Be Bearable

The other side of this same coin is important as well. In order for your spouse to bear with all things with you, you must be easy to bear. Strive to love them by giving them as little weight as possible to bear. Some people are so difficult to live with that they make the bearing all things unusually difficult. Concentrate on being bearable. Strive to live such a life that you are easy to lift.

Perhaps you do not know the ways you need to improve to be more bearable. I'd suggest that you sit down again with your spouse and be open to hearing the areas in which you must be more bearable. There is space at the end of this study for that type of evaluation. Life offers enough pressures and challenges on its own; we should try to cut down on as many things as possible.

15. Love Never Fails.

What a wonderful ending to this list of character traits! In our "all-inclusive" attributes of love we must remember that love never fails. Love bears all things (protects), believes and hopes all things, endures (remains under) all things, and never fails. When the banks of this world fail, our relationships must remain strong. When our extended family turns their back on us, we must be there to bear each other up. You must always be there for your husband or wife.

The beauty of this final attribute of love is that it so clearly reflects our Heavenly Father's love toward us. This idea brings us full circle to the beginning of our study. We began by considering how important it is in marriage for each spouse to be a born-again believer. This is not just referring to a denominational preference. Being born anew, being made alive spiritually, allows a person to mirror the God who gave them this birth. The Holy Spirit goes in and allows that person to take on the fruit of His character. One of those fruit is this fruit of faithfulness. Faithfulness in love never fails, and that is the way God acts towards His children. Those who know Jesus as Savior know that His love is an unending torrent of immeasurable love. His covenant to us is without change.

This is the love that we must show toward our spouse. Feelings come and go, but the faithful love must remain. Your desires and wishes may change, but acting toward the well-being of your spouse must not change.

Can you "Fall out of Love?"

I still remember Greg Mazak, a counseling teacher, saying, "You can fall out of a tree, but you cannot fall out of love." Sad to say, people use "falling out of love" as an excuse to try and end their marriage, what is intended as a permanent relationship.

> *Love is a choice. you can choose not to love,*
> *but you cannot fall out of love.*

However, this demonstrates a faulty understanding of the biblical concept of love. Love is not a feeling or an emotion. Love is a constant activity. Therefore, love is a choice. You can choose not to love, but you cannot "fall" out of love. This passage teaches us that love never fails. If that is the case, then you can love someone even when you don't feel like it. You can love someone even when your emotions say that you do not love them.

If you feel like you have fallen out of love, then let me encourage you to start loving your spouse even if you don't feel like it. God designed the emotions of love (mistakenly used as synonyms for love) to come *after* the actions of love. Don't wait for the "feeling" of love to act; you may be waiting for a long, long time.

Conclusion

These fifteen activities of love are extremely practical and should be reviewed regularly. Let me encourage you to take one evening a year to reevaluate where you are in your relationship as a loving person according to 1 Corinthians 13. In the back of this book, you will find a worksheet that walks through each of these activities of love and helps you fill out areas where you need to improve. This communication is essential to a marriage!

If you evaluate yourself and your relationships regularly, you will be able to communicate in a non-threatening way. You will not be dealing with the problem in the heat of the moment but in a regular checkup. Let me encourage you to take this checkup once a year together. Perhaps make it a fun weekend away, or at least an evening out.

What you do not work to maintain will soon become weak. Every relationship takes constant work. You cannot get lazy but should always strive to show more characteristics of love in your relationships. Keep well-maintained bridges in life!

∾

Chapter 4 Homework

1. What personal habits make being married to you "unbearable" or at least add unnecessary pressure to your spouse?

2. What are some ways that your spouse can build trust with you?

3. What are ways you would like for your spouse to protect you in the following three categories?

- Physically
- Emotionally
- Spiritually

4. The believer's mindset about marriage is that there is no room for divorce because love never .

COMMUNICATING IN LOVE

Loving

Biblical Principles for Developing
& Maintaining Loving Relationships

When Sarah and I were newly married, we sat down near a much older couple in a restaurant. They were speaking loud enough for us to catch about every word, so we overheard a bit too much of their communication, at least too much for our own comfort. What we really found interesting is that this couple talked together, but they did not communicate at all. They had two separate conversations with themselves on two separate topics with no interaction of ideas mixed from one or the other. It was fascinating! They talked nicely to one another, which was good, but they did not communicate.

Correct communication is critical to any relationship. If you don't talk openly and lovingly, you will constantly be frustrated in your marriage and in all of your interpersonal  contact with others. The Lord gives us a warning as He shares the power of communication, and He gives some practical rules for maintaining proper communication. In the following pages, we will examine the power of and guidelines for proper communication.

The Power of Communication

James 3:6-8 sets the tone for this chapter:

> "And the tongue is a fire, the very world of iniquity; the tongue is set among our members as that which defiles the entire body, and sets on fire the course of our life, and is set on fire by hell. For every species of beasts and birds, of reptiles and creatures of the sea, is tamed and has been tamed by the human race. But no one can tame the tongue; it is a restless evil and full of deadly poison."

There is so much power in your tongue – whether it is a blogging tongue, a texting tongue, a facebooking tongue, or a shooting the breeze over a coffee tongue. It is a fire and needs to be managed and controlled by you.

Consider another Scripture:

> "Set a guard, O LORD, over my mouth; Keep watch over the door of my lips" (Psalm 141:3).

David recognized that a power this great needed some regulation. David set armored soldiers about his mouth (figuratively, of course). He wanted some soldiers to stand guard and keep him from saying things improperly. These soldiers stand ready to put a sword through any improper communication before it escapes. Fiery words are blocked before they can burn anyone.

The following principles are practical "soldiers." Before we speak, we must make sure

 that the speech is proper. Of course the four lessons we have had on love apply generally to communication. We could apply them to all of our communication, but we want to take a lesson and survey passages in Scripture that deal with the topic of communication in particular.

You may recall from our first chapter that each person is like an island that builds bridges of communication to other islands. These soldiers act like border control agents that carefully inspect all the communication cargo that leaves our island for another island.

These agents check everything that goes out and comes in; they make sure that whatever goes out meets the standards for loving communication so that you will influence others for right.

Think of this in light of church relationships. We enjoy such a variety of connections with a variety of people in one body. The way you interact, the cargo you send, and the way in which you send it will either build up or tear down this body of believers. You must be extremely careful about what you send and how you send packages.

If you are avant-garde about your procedures – if you don't set the biblical principles of communication in your midst – then you will blow up more than bridges. Your cargo will spread like fire and burn up others as well. Some individuals are like this, although I don't know if they realize it or not. They go from church to church setting fires to bridges and islands. This is not good; in fact, it is scary! Their behavior throws a shadow on their claim of salvation.

We can apply the same thing to a marriage. What is it like to live with a fire-breathing dragon? Not very fun! So, let's be careful to tame that tongue and establish a proper set of regulations for our border control agents. Let's consider some biblical principles of cargo inspection.

The Rules of Communication

First Rule – Speak Truthfully

We will turn now to the practical letter that Paul wrote to the church in Ephesus that describes the worthy walk of a Christian in our communication habits. We glean these principles of proper communication from Chapter 4.

> "As a result, we are no longer to be children, tossed here and there by waves and carried about by every wind of doctrine, by the trickery of men, by craftiness in deceitful scheming; but speaking the truth in love, we are to grow up in all aspects into Him who is the head, even Christ" (Ephesians 4:14-15).

So the first rule about what you say is that you must be truthful. Consider a few other proverbs that state the same principle:

> "A false witness will perish, But the man who listens to the truth will speak forever" (Proverbs 21:28).

> "A false witness will not go unpunished, And he who tells lies will not escape" (Proverbs 19:5).

"A man who bears false witness against his neighbor is like a war club, or a sword, or a sharp arrow" (Proverbs 25:18).

Don't Lie

What does it mean to speak truthfully? Don't Lie. We could define lying as *intentionally communicating deception with evil intent*. Let's look at each component of that definition.

Intentional

The first attribute of a lie is that it is intentional. Once when interviewing for a job, I was asked about the amount of years working somewhere. I answered three years; it was something like that. As I thought about it later, I realized that it was actually four years... It was a fairly trivial fact in the whole scheme of things, but my conscience would not let me get away with it. So I called up the interviewer and confessed, "I'm so sorry, I said three but I should have said four; I didn't mean to deceive you."

I had not lied. I had stated the wrong information but not with intent. Now, depending on the factors involved, even that is something you will need to clear up. The intent to deceive is one major factor in lying.

It is not just that you misspoke. You will have to judge that carefully, however! "I said I graduated from Harvard, when it was actually a technical school... but I just completely misspoke... my bad!" No, that is not misspeaking; that is lying.

This includes more than just speaking. Communication today can take place in so many ways! This is when you text someone and say that you are almost there, but in reality you just got your things together.

Deception

The second aspect of lying is deception. You are causing them to misbelieve something about you or the circumstances around your communication. This includes exaggeration and hiding facts the other person should know.

I wonder what we would find out if we looked at the enrollment of Ivy League schools compared with those who state they are currently attending Ivy Leagues schools on their social media profile. Not everyone is attending these schools; it simply is not possible. Be careful to be genuine even online.

A little white lie is still a lie, and God hates lying. If you are distorting the facts to your advantage, you are lying. Let us be vigilant in this area in our homes. Don't be tempted to be loose with the facts. Be careful to tell the truth, the whole truth, and nothing but the truth.

So, lying is deceptive communication. Well, the weather channel engages in this nearly every day. Therefore, we must bring up one more component.

With Malice (with selfish or ill-intended motive)

This final factor completes our definition. Lying is given with an intent to deceive that profits you or affects another negatively. You have something to gain either for yourself or take from them by withholding or distorting the facts. You may have situations where you communicate your weight, and you know you are exaggerating (or minimizing) for your own benefit. You don't really weigh that much – you are exaggerating.

Perhaps you are told to organize a surprise birthday party. As soon as you agree to a surprise for someone, you are distorting the truth every time you meet with them because you are withholding facts from them. In this case, it is for their good, not to their detriment. This is not lying. We may want to be careful not to give them an answer that goes directly against the truth ("I won't see you tonight."), but you may withhold facts in order to hide the surprise. Again, that is not the sin of lying.

Speak the Truth

At times, it is much easier to say nothing. Perhaps in Christian circles this is what we struggle with more than anything. We want to avoid conflicts.

Perhaps you have seen the show "What Would You Do?" Many episodes have to do with whether or not you would speak up in a given situation, and some of them are just horrible. In one episode, an attractive young lady is robbing a very old man of a home, and she is pressuring him to marry her for his money. When the older individual struggles away from the table, who will confront the lady? Well, many did not. It is hard to speak the truth.

In Christian relationships, failing to communicate about something is at times worse than saying the wrong thing. We need to have open communication. Speak truthfully and use the following principles. But you don't have the option not to talk about it. You must communicate.

Reasons to Speak the Truth

Why should I speak truthfully? Well, God tells us to in His Word, so that should be enough. However, consider a few other reasons. Space does not permit us to go into these in detail, but I encourage you to take time to read the passages and consider their truths.

1. Speak the truth to reflect the character of our God (Hebrews 6:18; Titus 1:2).
2. Speak the truth because deception breeds further deception (Sin breeds sin; 2 Samuel 11).
3. Speak the truth because this is the way God has planned to build up His church (Speaking the truth in love = edification; Ephesians 4:14-16).

Second Rule – Speak Graciously

If I were to guess a percentage, I would have to say that 100% of divorces are caused in some measure by poor communication. Although communication is a wonderful asset to a relationship, it may also be a horrible liability. Loose lips sink ships, right? Well, loose lips sink marriages as well. Often the problem does not come from what is said, but how it is said. Be very careful how you say things!

Let's think carefully about the instruction in Ephesians when talking about putting on right communication:

"Let no unwholesome word proceed from your mouth, but only such a word as is good for edification according to the need of the moment, so that it will give grace to those who hear. Do not grieve the Holy Spirit of God, by whom you were sealed for the day of redemption. Let all bitterness and wrath and anger and clamor and slander be put away from you, along with all malice. Be kind to one another, tender-hearted, forgiving each other, just as God in Christ also has forgiven you" (Ephesians 4:29-32).

Let's consider a few components to speaking graciously. We need to incorporate the right tone, the right emphasis, the right time, the right place, and the right person.

The Right Tone

"A gentle answer turns away wrath, But a harsh word stirs up anger" (Proverbs 15:1).

"The Lord's bond-servant must not be quarrelsome, but be kind to all, able to teach, patient when wronged, with gentleness correcting those who are in opposition, if perhaps God may grant them repentance leading to the knowledge of the truth, and they may come to their senses and escape from the snare of the devil, having been held captive by him to do his will." (2 Timothy 2:24-26)

"The tongue of the wise makes knowledge acceptable, But the mouth of fools spouts folly" (Proverbs 15:2).

We have examined this idea of speaking the truth. The first principle must be to speak truthfully. However speaking the truth is not always enough. We must "speak the truth in love." Have the right tone! The way you say what you say should be considered kind. Would you describe your communication as light and easy or as heavy and harsh? Harsh communication is speaking in an improper tone.

You can be told that you are going to hell in such a way that you are not offended in the slightest, and you can be told that you have a spot of lunch on your shirt in such a way that you are extremely offended. The difference is not the subject matter but the tone with which you are told this.

We all notice when someone else is speaking in the wrong tone. One of the harshest forms of punishment for me is when I have to watch a few minutes of one of these shows where people come out and sing, dance, or perform in some way, and afterward three or four people judge them. It is not my cup of tea as far as preferences go. That being said, what I've learned in the few ones I've seen is that there is usually one judge that will say mean things – or at least honest things – and two that are just there to say nice things. This seems to be the shtick of how they design these programs. But usually the most honest person is the one saying the negative things to the cute little girl that is singing her heart out... as the crowd yells and screams. Usually that judge is correct, but they just don't let the person down lightly. Their tone is too in your face.[1]

I guess this is one thing that New Yorkers are good at. But it is not a good thing to be good at. You should be skilled both at speaking the truth and at making people receptive to that truth.

There is never a reason to yell at your spouse. Unless your spouse is in immediate physical danger, or you are trying to get their attention from across a long distance, you should not yell. This is rule #1 in speaking graciously. In every culture, yelling at someone is disrespectful and hurt-

ful. Yelling is out of bounds in every marriage. We must put
off the works of the flesh – namely harsh speech.

The Right Emphasis (Accompanying Gestures)

As we considered in a previous lesson, this includes
more than the words coming from your mouth. Your
nonverbal communication from your body is equally important. One example would be invading someone's personal
space by getting in their face. You may reason, "Well, I didn't
yell!" Yes, but getting right in their face is essentially the
same thing.

The Right Time

"A man has joy in an apt answer, and how delightful is a
timely word" (Proverbs 15:23)!

"Let no unwholesome word proceed from your mouth, but
only such a word as is good for edification according to the
need of the moment, so that it will give grace to those who
hear" (Ephesians 4:29).

We must wait for the proper time to talk with someone.
When someone is grieving over a loved one, it is best to just
sit and grieve with them, not confront them because they
lack faith in the second coming. We must be willing to give
people space at that time.

The same is true in a marriage relationship. Be careful
not to unload on your spouse the second you meet with
them. Give some time to let them unwind.

Waiting for the correct time in speaking also includes
being careful not to interrupt someone else. We don't speak

while someone is speaking. We wait for them to finish and then speak. Interrupting someone is rude, unloving speech.

These principles are simple, yet they are often simply ignored. Because they are not followed, relationships deteriorate and sour.

The Right Place

> "Like apples of gold in settings of silver Is a word spoken in right circumstances" (Proverbs 25:11).

Keep in secret what should be kept in secret. I remember sitting in a coffee shop one night, and two people plopped right down beside me talking about a legal case of liability. This lady wanted this or that and was asking this lawyer what to say, and she was getting very worked up! I really felt awkward and put my headphones on to try and give them some privacy. This happens too often!

If you have a question or concern of a sensitive nature, wait until you are in private. Don't publicly confront the person in front of many people. Married couples should also be careful to avoid debating in public, especially with children present. You may not be yelling, but your interaction can clearly come across as unloving. We can always wait until later when the time is right, and we are just with one another.

The Right Person

Also, especially in matters of confrontation, the communication should come from the right person. Be careful about confronting another person's children or family off the cuff. It is often better to talk to another family member who is closer to the situation and knows all of the details, and then perhaps you can bridge the subject together.

Going around and correcting everyone you see is not a spiritual gift; it is carnality. When we exhort, we must exhort in love – the right person, the right place, and the right time. Beyond these factors, we must do so in the right tone, speaking only the truth.

Third Rule – Put Off Loveless Speech

In Ephesians 4 and 5, we are told not only the type of speech to put *on*, but also the type of speech to put *off*. We don't have the space to go into all of these in depth, but let's at least read through them to make sure they are not a part of our communication habits.

> "And there must be no filthiness and silly talk, or coarse jesting, which are not fitting, but rather giving of thanks. For this you know with certainty, that no immoral or impure person or covetous man, who is an idolater, has an inheritance in the kingdom of Christ and God" (Ephesians 5:4-5).

Filthiness

This is the only time this word is used in the New Testament. It has reference to shamefulness, obscenity, and baseness in speech. It represents filthy speech. We must put off words that are filthy. There are whole classes of words and topics that should just be completely put off. This would include cursing and what is considered foul language or four letter words. These are unloving.

Silly Talk

The word translated silly talk is interesting. It too occurs only here in the entire New Testament. It is a compound word made up of two other words. One of the words is the word "to speak." The second term is the Greek term from which we get our word "moron." So it is moronic speech or moronic words – speech that is nonsense and is not for edification. It is just blathering silly foolishness for selfishness sake. John MacArthur defines it this way:

> "Stupid talk, talk only befitting someone who is intellectually deficient. It is sometimes referred to as low obscenity, foolish talk that comes from the drunk or the gutter mouth. It has no point except to give an air of dirty worldliness."[2]

Coarse Jesting

The third type of speech is similar. It is low jesting. This refers to making jokes with double meaning or crude humor. Most humor occurs just using the element of surprise. From peek-a-boo with your infant to slapstick comedy, the laugh comes with the surprise, the unexpected punch line. That surprise strikes you as unexpected and makes you laugh.

Coarse jesting is using filthy situations and ideas to shock people to laughter. It makes up the majority of content in modern sitcoms.

These three types of speech are improper and just don't fit for someone that is a believer. What are we to do with these three types of speech? Eliminate them. These are not fitting. These are not proper, so they should be put off. Once we become a believer, there is no place for this type of communication.

I enjoy the biography of Brother Andrew. He grew up in Holland and lived a life as a rather rough soldier until he came to know the Lord as Savior. After his conversion so many things changed in his life. Quickly he desired more and more to share this good news with others. Once brother Andrew submitted to the Lord's leading in his life, he said he would be a missionary anywhere.

And so he began – where he was. He got a job at a huge industrial chocolate plant nearby – where he wanted to be a light to the people and share Jesus with them. However, it was not as easy as he expected. His first day on the job, he was ushered through a maze of hallways and corridors into a large packaging area. This is where about 200 women worked packaging the chocolates before they were shipped out in the next area.

This was his post, and he was greeted with a room full of whistles and off-color sexual comments. He said that even his years in the military did not prepare him for the language he heard that morning. Let's listen as he picks up the story in his own words: "The leader of the foul wise-cracking, I discovered, was a girl named Greetje. I was grateful when my cart was full and I could escape for a few moments to what seemed like the sanctuary of male company in the shipping room."

Daily he was bombarded with this woman's foul mouth and wisecracks. She controlled the moral tone and perver-sity of the entire company of women. But he and another Christian began ministering even under these conditions.

They would pick them up and bus them to a Gospel meeting nearby, until finally things came to a climax. Brother Andrew was ministering to a lady who was blind with notes he would write in braille. He would share the Gospel and the answer to all her deepest problems in Jesus. Greetje picked up on the notes and publicly exposed this in her normal distasteful way. Andrew stood up to her – 'Shut up. . . The bus for church leaves Saturday morning at 9. I want you on it!' There was silence.

And she agreed. More silence followed as the ladies went back to work. Saturday came and Greetje was on the bus! She joked through the entire meeting – using foul speech and making obscene jokes to the preaching.

Andrew took her home without really challenging her – just being kind in his speech and considerate in his demeanor. That kindness she said killed her. She wondered if perhaps she had gone too far for God to reach her. She cried out to God for mercy and forgiveness – and He forgave her. And He changed her. The next day Andrew and the other believers were in for a huge surprise! Greetje's mouth was stopped.

'People asked – "What on earth did you say to her? Something terrific happened!' All morning long Greetje did not crack one dirty joke. And once a lady dropped a box of chocolates . . . instead of her blasting her, she was the one that reached down and helped her pick up the pieces. What a change! What a testimony!

Did this lady do this to be saved? Did she clean up her life in order to be saved? No! She realized that she needed to be rescued. She could not save herself. And so she called on Jesus for salvation. And then God saved her – and changed her from the inside out.[3]

This is something that shocked me a bit when I moved to NYC (the price of rent? well, yes that is shocking too). I was really surprised at people's language. I worked a secular job while spending a couple of years in Brooklyn as a youth pastor, yet I heard the same horrible language from children on the street speaking to their mother. And yet all of society is taking this route, not just urban centers. Consequently, this is yet another way for us to be salt and light as we put off improper communication with all others, both believers and unbelievers, and put on the Words of Christ.

> "Let your speech always be with grace, as though seasoned with salt, so that you will know how you should respond to each person" (Colossians 4:6).

One more quick note of instruction from Ephesians 5, and we will have to draw this topic to a close. What does the Lord tell us at the close of the section in Ephesians 5? When we put off corrupt communication, we replace it with something else. We replace it with thanksgiving. Let's not take our relationships for granted, but openly thank one another.

> "And there must be no filthiness and silly talk, or coarse jesting, which are not fitting, but rather giving of thanks" (Ephesians 5:4).

A Practical Plan for Communication

A counselor that I respect highly used the following to help couples communicate through differences. He asked them to place a stone on the table in front of them both and act as if that was the problem or issue that needed discussion.

Because each of us has a different view of every problem or situation, it is best to get each person's view of the rock from their side.

At this point each person is able to communicate their view. They should communicate the facts as well as how they feel about the problem or how the problem or circumstances makes them feel.

I like this idea and have adapted it a little in counseling people who have an interpersonal conflict. Instead of a rock (I do believe some of the couples I have counseled would use the rock in ways that are completely unintended by me!), I use a notebook. I get a nice looking communication notebook – something like a journal. Then I ask each person to write the problem in his or her own words on a page of the notebook. Each person should describe their view of the problem vocally with the notebook with the problem written on it in between them. We are now focusing on the problem written there, not the person sitting on the other side of the problem.

This communication should be under control and follow the rules of communication outlined above. Whenever someone wants to communicate about a problem or a large issue in the relationship, they can retrieve the notebook, write down the problem, and request communication from all parties involved.

The rules of communication included in this chapter will need to be developed into proper habits. Communication is such a pervasive part of our lives that these rules must become second nature to you. That is the way to develop consistent victory in this powerful area.

Chapter 5 Homework

1. Define lying:

2. Which of these is not considered lying based on our definition of lying?

- Plagiarism
- Tax Evasion
- Understating your weight.
- Forgetfully telling someone the wrong year for your high school graduation.

3. You have a friend that is a pathological liar. It seems that they are always stretching the truth or leading you astray with their words. They have become a believer and opened up to you with their need to change. How would you counsel them?

4. Samuel purposefully deceived Saul in I Samuel 16, but it was not sin (True / False).

5. What are ways to speak truth to your friends and acquaintances (think of what to put off and put on)?

6. Identify the rule of communication that has been broken in each circumstance below (A - Speak truthfully; B - Speak graciously; C - Put off loveless speech).

- When asked to put down their video game, the child responded by yelling, "You are so controlling!" _____
- Jimbob tells Nancy and their entire class that she should get some help from a tutor or something because she scored a 20 on the midterm exam.

  _____

- Your friend always has a witty comment to add quietly under his breath that may be funny but is usually off-color. _____
- After asking three times to no avail, Jimbob finally loses it and screams at his 12-year-old to go get him a coke. _____
- Jimbob's boss asked him why he called in sick and he mentioned that he had a headache, but forgot to mention that he was able to make it to a doubleheader Met's Yankees game. _____

FORGIVING IN LOVE

s you have gone through the previous chapters,
certainly you have been awakened by the truth
that you are not doing everything perfectly. Every
time I go over these principles, I'm reminded again of yet
another way that I have been unloving. What do we do
then? That is what this lesson is about. We will all do things
that displease our spouse, friend, co-worker, or family
member, so we must learn the art of forgiveness.

The opposite of forgiveness in your heart is bitterness,
and there are few deadlier influences in someone's life than
a bitter spirit.

The Lord commands:

> "Let all bitterness and wrath and anger and clamor and
> slander be put away from you, along with all malice"
> (Ephesians 4:31).

If we allow a bitter spirit to fester, it will ruin the relationship. It is like drinking battery acid. You will not be able
to stomach it very long, and it

will end up eating you on the inside. So let's look below at the steps toward forgiveness and the motivation for forgiveness, both taught by Jesus.

> "If your brother sins, go and show him his fault in private; if he listens to you, you have won your brother. But if he does not listen to you, take one or two more with you, so that by the mouth of two or three witnesses every fact may be confirmed" (Matthew 18:15-16).

Let's follow the stages or steps of forgiveness as outlined in Jesus' teaching in this passage.

Steps Toward Forgiveness

Step One – An Offense

Step number one is an offense. This seems obvious, but let's not pass over it. Plenty of people are very good at giving an offense, right? But remember two primary principles of love: love does not take into account a wrong suffered, and love is patient.

Let's do our best to stop the process at this point. Perhaps you can give the person space to sin against you and not feel any bitterness or resentment toward them. You know how much you have already been forgiven, and you know that you could easily be guilty of the same thing. So instead of flying off the handle at them, you are patient and soon forget all about it.

The process ends there. You don't approach them unless

you believe it would be best for them to hear how they might offend someone else. As loving people, let's let the offense stop here, with my not taking offense. Peter said this about love:

> "Above all, keep fervent in your love for one another, because love covers a multitude of sins" (I Peter 4:8).

It may stop there. You were inadvertently tripped, and instead of ripping the person's head off for leaving their cane in the way, you forget about it. And you truly do. There is no bitterness there because you do not think about it again.

But what if you do think about it again? Then you must start to communicate the offense with the person who offended you.

What must you do? Well, you move on to the next step and that is to communicate. Before we do move on to that stage, let's make a couple clarifications.

What is an offense?

The word most often translated *offense* in Scripture is not the same as our word in English. The English word *offense* can be used at any point for any reason. If I wear deodorant I may offend someone who thinks this causes cancer, and if I don't I can offend even more people, for ... well for obvious reasons. The Greek word is a little stronger.

It has reference to *causing someone to stumble* and not usually physically but spiritually. Your actions may cause someone to stumble into sin. The word is used in the passage where Jesus teaches that if your eye causes you to stumble (causes offense), then pluck it out! The idea is you are leading someone to sin. However, it is also used when Jesus encouraged His disciples to pay the temple tax, which  they really were not required to pay if they wanted to push their rights. In order to not offend the temple officials, He encouraged them to pay the tax (by getting the money from the mouth of a fish).

This is an important clarification. We need to be mature believers so that we are not put out of sorts or worse yet, bitter for a small thing like someone not speaking with us at church. There is an endless list of small things that we should really not put into the category of offenses that our society may put in that category. Let's try to live in such an inoffensive way, and try to be so patient with others, that it is rare for us to truly offend another person. When the confrontation comes, it will be more like what Jesus states in Matthew 17 – it is a definite sin that we must bring up for the help of our brother or sister.

What if I'm trying to forget?

But what about if you are not sure? There is something, perhaps of a smaller nature that offends you, and you are committed to letting it pass, but you are not sure if you can. What should you do? In a previous lesson, we used the rule of thumb given in Ephesians 4.

"Be angry, and yet do not sin; do not let the sun go down on your anger" (Ephesians 4:26).

If someone offends you but you forget about it easily in just a few hours, it is in this category that we can allow love to cover. However, if 24 hours have passed then you really better get to communication, or you are in danger of falling into bitterness, which will ruin the relationship as well as your fellowship with the Lord.

Step Two – Communicate

Communication is essential at this point. Both the offended and the offender must communicate. The offended must communicate what has offended them. The offender must apologize and ask for forgiveness. Remember to follow the rules!

The offended person must communicate.

> "If your brother sins, go and show him his fault in private;
> if he listens to you, you have won your brother."

The offended person is required to communicate the offense to the person who has offended them. We should not leave them to guess, nor should we get bitter. As we discovered in a previous lesson, often we are tempted when offended to either clam up or blow up; or worse yet, clam up until we blow up.

This is so unhealthy. If you wait 24 hours and cannot forget, you must communicate your offense. You cannot keep it inside you. This is asking for a bitter spirit. These are your options: communicate with the offender, forget in love, or become bitter toward them.

The root of bitterness affects you spiritually. It is a sin.

However, it often spreads from you to others. Your bitter spirit, thrown into the pot of a bunch of other Christians can make them bitter as well.

Even if you don't believe the person will apologize and ask for forgiveness, that is not your responsibility. You are to communicate the offense. You must approach them and mention that their action toward you has offended you.

The offending person must communicate.

Once the offense has been communicated to the offender, then the offender must take seriously the accusation, apologize, and request forgiveness. This should be verbalized, not implied. "I'm so sorry that I offended you when I said that about you. I assure you that I was merely joking, but I see how my joke was in bad taste. Please forgive me for being offensive."

> "Therefore if you are presenting your offering at the altar, and there remember that your brother has something against you, leave your offering there before the altar and go; first be reconciled to your brother, and then come and present your offering" (Matthew 5:23-24).

This passage connects offended relationships with worship. If we have offended someone – you know they have something against you – you must get it right with them before you go to worship. You are affected in your horizontal relationship to God if you are not right in your vertical relationships with others.

Step Three – Release and Reconciliation

Once forgiveness is requested, it must be given. How many times in one day should we forgive someone of the same offense? Two times? Three times? Jesus said 499 times for the same offense, and we are still required to forgive (Matt. 18:22). That is impossible without God's enabling grace, and yet it is required. Bitterness, lingering resentment is not an option for a Christian.

When you forgive someone you are *releasing* them from that offense. You no longer hold it between you and them. They are free. That means that you do not bring it up again. You can no longer catalog that offense.

Will you forget the offense as soon as you forgive? Well, no, you will not. You cannot forget immediately. But when you forgive, you are promising not to bring it up against them again. The negative feelings may stay for a little while, but if you choose to release them and communicate your forgiveness, then the healing starts immediately. Eventually your feelings will follow your choice to obey.

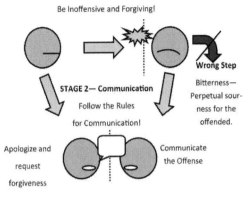

STAGE 1— Offence

Be Inoffensive and Forgiving!

Wrong Step

Bitterness— Perpetual sourness for the offended.

STAGE 2— Communication

Follow the Rules

for Communication!

Apologize and request forgiveness

Communicate the Offense

STAGE 3— Release and Restore

Offended releases the offended of the offense, and restores relationship.

Once forgiveness is granted, we pick up the relationship where it was before the offense. This is *restoration*. Bringing the offense up repeatedly at a later time is not an option. That is tempting, but we must remember that true love is a horrible accountant. It fails to take record of the offenses done.

A question regarding restoration often arises when someone has betrayed a trust. If a person betrays a trust, should everything return to normal once all is forgiven? That is not possible in many cases. If a child takes the family car, rides recklessly, and totals the vehicle, all may be forgiven, but there will be a time of waiting before he is able to gain the trust back. In love, the family will provide safeguards so that the same error does not occur. The same is true in a case where a spouse has been unfaithful. Although he or she may be forgiven, the loving spouse will provide safeguards to help keep the same sin from reoccurring. This is not un-forgiveness but love that guards another from sin.

Motivation for Forgiveness

Jesus' parable of the unjust servant truly gives us a proper motivation for forgiveness:

"For this reason the kingdom of heaven may be compared to a king who wished to settle accounts with his slaves. When he had begun to settle them, one who owed him ten thousand talents was brought to him. But since he did not have the means to repay, his lord commanded him to be sold, along with his wife and children and all that he had, and repayment to be made. So the slave fell to the ground and prostrated himself before him, saying, 'Have patience with me and I will repay you everything.' And the lord of that slave felt compassion and released him and forgave him the debt. But that slave went out and found one of his fellow slaves who owed him a hundred denarii; and he seized him and began to choke him, saying, 'Pay back what you owe.' So his fellow slave fell to the ground and began to plead with him, saying, 'Have patience with me and I will repay you.' But he was unwilling and went and threw him in prison until he should pay back what was owed. So when his fellow slaves saw what had happened, they were deeply grieved and came and reported to their lord all that had happened. Then summoning him, his lord said to him, 'You wicked slave, I forgave you all that debt because you pleaded with me. 'Should you not also have had mercy on your fellow slave, in the same way that I had mercy on you?' And his lord, moved with anger, handed him over to the torturers until he should repay all that was owed him. My heavenly Father will also do the same to you, if each of you does not forgive his brother from your heart" (Matthew 18:23-35).

How can you and I pray for forgiveness if we are still holding back forgiveness from someone else? In this parable, Jesus teaches that it is impossible. The conclusion is that if you are holding back this release from others, you are not truly a disciple. You are not a follower of Jesus, and as such you do not have forgiveness yourself. A forgiven person forgives. If you have been forgiven a lifetime of sin, then you definitely need to forgive others.

When we consider the deep pain that others cause in our lives, it is very difficult to forgive as Jesus did. He was able to look at those who were torturing Him and forgive them. The forgiveness that is ours is not something we make ourselves able to give; it is Christ in us. It is the ability that only He can give. If you struggle with forgiveness, ask the Lord to enable you to release that person who has harmed you. Holding them under your bitterness does nothing but affect you, so release them and serve the Lord.

Ever since the deaths of Jesus and Stephen, the first Christian martyr, true believers have had to forgive people from some of the greatest hurts. One such person is Jo Pollard.

Jo and her husband Michael were schoolteachers in New Zealand and gave their summers to taking trips to the Ukraine, Romania, and other closed communist countries to bring aid and Gospel literature. They did this for 27 summers, and the stories that they tell of how the Lord used them are really touching. In 1997 they crossed into Eastern Europe through Britain to Holland, eventually to the Czech Republic, Slovakia, and then to Hungary.

During their first night in Hungary, Jo heard a loud

knock at the back door of their travel camper. A man flashed an ID card and said he was with the police; however, she thought he was too young to be with the police. He yelled back that they were in an illegal spot and needed to pay a fine. She woke up Michael, and they moved the camper. In an hour, it happened again. This time Michael took the wheel and started preparing to drive away. Before he had a chance to start the vehicle, someone broke through the driver side window and beat him in the head with a crowbar. The burglar beat him repeatedly right in front of Jo. She started screaming for help, and the man ran away.

She started trying to help resuscitate her husband to no avail. Michael passed into eternity right in front of her. She did not know what to do. She decided to wait until morning to drive for help. She took all of the valuables except 50 pounds and hid the rest just in case they came back. She sat waiting with insect spray at hand beside her husband's dead body. They did return that night and beat Jo unconscious breaking her jaw and nose in two places. She was left unconscious to die, and three men took valuables from their van.

The event that caught world news was what Jo said while she recovered in the hospital. She was given an interview by a local station from her bedside – with her face swollen and her body still racked with pain. A microphone was placed in front of her face, and she was asked to say a few words. She replied:

"I have been told that my attackers have been caught. Three of them, one aged 18 and two 22-year-olds. I don't know what their sentence will be. I don't feel any malice towards them because I'm a Christian, and as such I just hope they realize that what they have done is wrong and against God's will and in time that they will be born again – become Christians themselves."

This was not just speech during the blur of a near death experience. Months later at the trial, she looked each of them in the eye and told them that she forgave them. She reached out to their parents having a son the same age and has become friends with the one of the mothers. When they each went to jail, the longest term being 11 years, she sent them presents in jail and Christian literature.[1]

That is forgiveness. That is Christianity, the life of a disciple. Again, it is not just difficult; this is impossible without a new nature, without being born again. Once we trust that Christ died in our place to forgive us of our sins, then we are given a new nature. This new nature is one that is spiritually alive and has the vitality to love as He loved, forgive as He forgave, and talk as He talked. This is the key to all relationships – being right with our Creator through Jesus Christ.

Lesson 6 Homework

1. What is the opposite of forgiveness?

2. What picture does the Bible use to describe bitterness? What does this picture teach?

3. Discussion Question – Consider the phrase, "For-

giving is forgetting." In what way is this true and in what way is it not true?

4. What is a primary motivation for forgiveness for a Christian?

FULFILLING YOUR ROLE IN LOVE PART 1

I n these final two chapters, we will consider love from a husband and wife standpoint. How can I fulfill the role that God has given me in my family? I would encourage you to read these chapters even if you are not married nor anticipate marriage in your near future. God's expectation for the family is a vital part of Christian teaching for families, churches, and our society in general. It is up to all of us to understand and support the biblical roles in marriage. Our society sure takes enough potshots at the biblical family at any chance that it can. Therefore, we must arm our minds with the right concept of family and do so based not on what is traditional or popular but based on what is revealed in Scripture.

The Maker of the Marriage Team

On a championship sports team, what often provides the greatest success is not having all the best players but having a solid team. These teammates know their role and

accomplish it in tandem with
their other teammates. Just as a
properly running sports team is
composed of athletes who fulfill
their roles well, properly
running marriages are

composed of two spouses who are committed to fulfilling
their roles in the family.

Of course the best way to gain an understanding of how
marriage roles work is to consult the Manufacturer of
marriage.

Let's say that someone got you a diet-shake-making-
gizmo for your wedding. You open it up as soon as you get
off the plane for your honeymoon because you are so
excited about this little diet-shake-making-gizmo-thing. But
it doesn't work. You are distraught! You were so looking
forward to using that little gizmo, and now you stand crying,
disappointed; your honeymoon is ruined.

But, in a flash the doorbell rings, and there is Maria
Encontes with her husband. She owns the gizmo company,
and he actually designed the very model that you are
holding in your hands. A smile breaks in on your face,
clashing with the tears in your eyes. Yes! He can fix it. And
he does.

That probably will not (or did not) happen on your
honeymoon, but it illustrates an important point. Although
this book can't fix everything about your marriage, it will
point you to the owner of the company, the inventor,
designer, and the one Person who put your exact model
marriage together. And that is Christ. So let's listen to what
He says about how to make marriage work smoothly.

Marriage is a God-ordained institution. As the architect,

He knows how marriages work best. We will consider first some principles from God's account at creation, then the majority of instruction from Paul's letter to the Ephesians.

- Marriage Principles from Creation
- Marriage Roles from Ephesians

Marriage Principles from Creation

Let's start by examining the first married couple. Adam and Eve were not a perfect example by any stretch of the imagination, but they are a married couple that received a marriage counseling session straight from God. It's best that we start there.

"Then the LORD God said, 'It is not good for the man to be alone; I will make him a helper suitable for him.' Out of the ground the LORD God formed every beast of the field and every bird of the sky, and brought them to the man to see what he would call them; and whatever the man called a living creature, that was its name. The man gave names to all the cattle, and to the birds of the sky, and to every beast of the field, but for Adam there was not found a helper suitable for him. So the LORD God caused a deep sleep to fall upon the man, and he slept; then He took one of his ribs and closed up the flesh at that place. The LORD God fashioned into a woman the rib which He had taken from the man, and brought her to the man. The man said, 'This is now bone of my bones, And flesh of my flesh; She shall be called Woman, Because she was taken out of Man.' For this reason a man shall leave his father and his mother, and be joined to his wife; and they shall become one flesh. And the man and his wife were both naked and were not ashamed" (Genesis 2:18-25).

The Principle of Companionship

A Problem

When God looked upon the garden that He had made, He looked at Adam and said something that was unexpected: "It is not good for the man to be alone." To this point everything had been good. If we look at the previous chapter of Genesis everything so far was good. Verse 4 ("God saw that the light was good."), verse 10 ("the gathering of the water He called seas; and God saw that it was good."), verse 12 ("The earth brought forth vegetation, plants yielding seed after their kind, and trees bearing fruit with seed in them, after their kind; and God saw that it was good."), and verses 16-18 ("God made the two great lights.... And God saw that it was good.") echo the same idea. Yet in chapter two God says that this situation is not good.

What is the problem? Man is alone. God made Adam to have communion. He is made in the image of the Trinity Who speaks in perfect communion together. So, how can man do this communion if he is alone? Another person must be found to have close companionship with Adam.

A Solution

The solution is not in the animal kingdom. Some wonder why Adam named the different animals of the garden at this time (2:20). It is probably because Adam needed to be shown that in God's creation there were no solutions to this problem. No one could share the intimacies of life with Adam. Dog is man's best friend, but God brought the animals around to show that nothing in creation to that point was "suitable."

We transition quickly to surgery, then poetry. God put Adam to sleep, took his rib, and formed the rib into a companion for Adam. Woman was made after man and made out of man. Woman (Hebrew, *isha*) means out of man (*ish*). The result was wonderful. In fact, when Adam saw her for the first time (especially after having seen all the animals), he burst out with the first poem in History.

> "This is now bone of my bones,
> And flesh of my flesh;
> She shall be called Woman,
> Because she was taken out of Man."

This shows that one of the primary functions of marriage is companionship. As Christians we need to work on this companionship over the years. We need to learn what our spouse enjoys and strive to enjoy that with them. In order for this to work best in life, both husband and wife must talk and communicate well with the other. Our eyes do this in order to see three dimensionally. "By using the visual images from both eyes, the brain can construct a 3D visual world that enables us to precisely judge the depth of objects."[1] As the husband and wife share the images of life together, their relationships and experiences deepen.

Companionship for the husband – As men, we tend to be off on our own. Like John Wayne we want to "go it alone." However, this is not a healthy role model for a husband. We need to recognize that God's purpose is not to remove ourselves into the dungeon of our own thoughts but to establish and develop a close companionship with our wives. We cannot be lazy in this endeavor. We must take the time to develop this relationship. When children come into the picture, we cannot allow their companionship to substitute for our spouse. We must pursue companionship for the entire marriage.

Companionship for the wife – We will develop the relationship between the two roles of the husband and wife much more fully from Ephesians 5, but this passage gives a clear definition of the companionship required of the wife. "I will make him a helper suitable for him." This is how God defines the role of a wife in a marriage relationship. She is to be a helper, and she is suitable to ("a perfect fit for") the husband. You are a helper to your husband. You are also designed to complete and match him. If there are ways you are not compatible, then it would be good to adapt and try to fit him completely (of course, Scripture gives parameters for what should or should not be adapted). How can you fit with your husband and help him in his goals in life? How can you complete him?

The Principle of Closeness

Closeness is communicated in several ways in this passage. First of all, woman was taken from man. They are of the same substance. This is the closest of relationships. Second, she was taken from his side, close to his heart, and under the strength of his arm. She is both cherished and protected, close to his side. Third, they were naked and unashamed. Fourth, there was nothing between them at all; this is pictured in the sexual relationship. God created man and woman to have a unique relationship where nothing should stand between them.

Woman was taken from Adam's side close to his heart. As a dating couple, a boyfriend and girlfriend will not allow anything to separate their time together. If distance is a problem, they will drive thousands of miles. They will stay up late at night talking on the phone to develop closeness. However, after years of marriage, the intimacy of marriage can wear off. We must work against this even if it is out of choice rather than desire. Just as we must choose to love our spouse, we must choose to be close to them. Think back on the things you did when dating and continue to act in this way.

The fact that they were naked and unashamed does not just speak to the physical intimacy between the husband and wife. It also speaks to the open transparency between husband and wife emotionally. We do not have hidden closets or bank accounts. We share all and keep no secrets. If we are one flesh, we cannot keep things from our spouse. The more you keep from them, the less you are open and one flesh with them.

The Principle of Permanence

Verse 24 gives us another important principle in the first marriage relationship.

> "For this reason a man shall leave his father and his mother, and be joined to his wife; and they shall become one flesh."

There is an important dynamic here. When a marriage is formed, a new entity develops. Two activities are included in this. These two activities are often described as "leaving" and "cleaving."

Leave

Both persons must leave their family. This is an interesting command, as the two did not have children yet – much less grandchildren. But God knew that a healthy marriage requires a new beginning. There must be a leaving of the two families. A new household must be set up. This is a wonderful creation – a new creation of a one-flesh union. I know of a parent who accompanied their son and new daughter–in-law on the honeymoon. This is extremely unhealthy! We all recognize that, but it is just as unhealthy to the marriage. A wife and a husband work best when someone else is not looking over their shoulders making suggestions.

Leaving a parent is not only just physically leaving, it includes an emotional cut as well. I have heard of spouses that call their parents and talk for an hour a night. This would be extremely difficult in a marriage. In order for you to be joined as companions, you must leave your family and join to your spouse. Your marriage is now your number one family relationship.

Cleave

The word cleave is a very strong word. This is a permanent bond that cannot be broken without serious damage. If you glue a vase together with crazy glue, the bond becomes stronger than the original piece. You cannot open the seal without breaking the vase. The same is true in marriage. You cannot break this marriage without seriously harming both persons.

Because marriage is a permanent bond, "divorce" cannot enter the vocabulary of a Christian couple. It should not happen. Having this perspective is essential, especially for those who are heading into marriage.

Another passage that speaks to the permanent nature of this cleaving (and the companionship) is Malachi 2:

> "Because the LORD has been a witness between you and
> the wife of your youth, against whom you have dealt

treacherously, though she is your companion and your wife by covenant. But not one has done so who has a remnant of the Spirit. And what did that one do while he was seeking a godly offspring? Take heed then to your spirit, and let no one deal treacherously against the wife of your youth. 'For I hate divorce,' says the LORD, the God of Israel, 'and him who covers his garment with wrong,' says the LORD of hosts. 'So take heed to your spirit, that you do not deal treacherously'" (Malachi 2:14-16).

From this passage we learn that God hates divorce. But there is an important word here that defines a marriage. In verse 14, God tells those in Israel who had divorced that they have dealt treacherously with their wife by covenant. This word covenant is a solemn word that is used of God's relationship with us. Marriage is not just a trial period. It is a "covenant between God and witnesses." This promise must not be taken lightly. Because covenants are permanent, marriage is permanent.

Are you committed to the permanency of your marriage? You are to display God's faithfulness to your spouse even if your spouse does not show the same back to you. A covenant is based not on the other person's actions but on your solemn promises before God.

I like to ask married couples or couples in pre-marriage counseling if they think there were ever a time they should murder their spouse. Almost always there are rather disgusting looks on their faces as they think of the word murder in the same sentence with this person that they have spent so much time. But, perhaps there would be a time when you were separated and both had to join opposing military units and were required to shoot down an enemy plane that was about to bomb your home base. And you did not know that your spouse was flying the enemy plane, so you did or had to... It is a little silly to think of the scenario when it might be ok to take the life of your spouse.

We should similarly recoil at the thought of divorce. That word should not enter our vocabulary. And so when someone asks when it is ok to divorce, I ask, when is it ok to kill your spouse? I can think of very few scenarios. Therefore, our commitment to this companionship should be very high! This is God's plan: one husband, one wife, for life.

Marriage Roles from Ephesians

As I consider trying to summarize what the Bible teaches about marriage roles in just one lesson, I'm overwhelmed. But then I consider that the Lord did just that to the church in Ephesus through the writing of the Holy Spirit through the Apostle Paul. So we too will walk through that passage. As we walk through the different roles (see next chapter for the specifics), let's begin with an overview of Paul's instruction to the Ephesian believers in their marriages, so we understand the context.

The Roles in Context

As we understand the role of a husband and a wife in a marriage relationship, we will remember the truth that we discovered when applying the principles of love. This is not just hard; this is impossible! It is impossible to fulfill without the Holy Spirit enabling us. We see this clearly in chapters 5 and 6 of Ephesians. Before we jump into the instruction to husbands and wives specifically in our next chapter, let's take a moment to point out more carefully how

God's Spirit gives strength to each spouse in the roles of both husband and wife.

The first three chapters of Ephesians are doctrinal, meaning they teach spiritual truths. They share with us the glory of being "in Christ." As Christians we have a huge number of spiritual blessings and these chapters delight us in those truths.

Incidentally, only one command is found in these three chapters. However, something radically changes in the tone of Ephesians beginning with Chapter 4. Here Paul begins to apply what he has taught. Because we are in Christ and therefore in the family of God, we must walk a certain way. We must walk in a way that best reflects our heavenly Father of our spiritual family.

> "Therefore I, the prisoner of the Lord, implore you to walk in a manner worthy of the calling with which you have been called" (Ephesians 4:1).

So, what kind of walk is worthy of our spiritual Father as children in this new family?

- First, the worthy walk is a walk of unity in the church (4:1-16).
- Second, the worthy walk is a walk of purity (4:17-32).
- Third, the worthy walk is a walk of love (5:1-5).
- Fourth, the worthy walk is a walk in light (5:6-13).
- Fifth, the worthy walk is a walk of wisdom (5:15-6:9).
- Last, the worthy walk is a walk of strength (6:10-20).

Under the fifth section, the walk of wisdom, Paul outlines how to be wise, namely, by being controlled by God's Spirit (5:18).

"So then do not be foolish, but understand what the will of the Lord is. And do not get drunk with wine, for that is dissipation, but be filled with the Spirit" (Ephesians 5:17-18).

The Lord then gives us a description of a Spirit-filled life. Someone who is controlled by God's Spirit will be someone who is (1) singing and (2) giving thanks. Then, the primary and final description of a Spirit-filled life is that we are (3) submitting – singing, thanking, and submitting.

"...submitting to one another out of reverence for Christ" (Ephesians 5:21)...

This submission is required of all of us one to another. Following this general command, Spirit-filled submission is applied to several relationships:

- Wives (5:22-24)
- Husbands (5:25-33)
- Children (6:1-3)
- Parents (6:4)
- Employers and employees (6:5-9)

We learn two principles from this instruction:
We will submit to one another all our lives.
At times we focus so much on one area of submission (the wife's role), that we don't realize that in context we are all submitting to one another. The husband submits to his

wife in love. Although he is the head of the family and will be the one responsible for the decisions made, his role of submission is one of selfless service toward the family with no thought of return. A servant doesn't assert his own will but instead submits his will to provide what others need.

The only way we can submit to one another consistently is by the power of God's Spirit.

The roles of both husband and wife can be carried out only as we are controlled by God's Spirit. God alone can do these things consistently, so we must constantly ask Him for grace to submit to one another in the fear of the Lord.

One final thought: when considering fulfilling your role in marriage, think of these three steps: Stop, Drop, and Control. This is extremely helpful advice when considering such an important relationship. We will all come through times when the only way to lovingly submit to one another will be by the power of God's Spirit. 1. Stop. 2. Drop. 3. Control.

Stop – When you feel your temper rising, or you feel like you are about to lose it, stop what you are doing. You may need to leave the room.

Drop – Drop to your knees; pray. You don't need to drop to your literal knees, but internally kneel in prayer. Confess your struggle in the situation and ask for help!

Control – Ask for God's Spirit to enable you. Ask the Lord to strengthen and enable you through His Spirit. Ask Him to take over.

～

Chapter 7 Homework

1. How can you become a more suitable companion?

2. What types of things do (did) you do when dating that helped you grow close to one another?

3. What was the first poem?

4. What is meant by "leaving" and "cleaving"?

FULFILLING YOUR ROLE IN LOVE PART 2

Loving

Biblical Principles for Developing
& Maintaining Loving Relationships

The blueprint, the map for a building project, is actually very valuable. I once saw on eBay that the blueprints for the S.C. Johnson Wax Buildings by Frank Lloyd Wright were on sale. Twenty-nine drawings on heavy paper including elevations, site plan, and floor plans were selling for $20,000! Another set of his blueprints were for the house called "Falling Waters," a house Wright designed for the Edward J. Kauffman family in 1936. The pre-auction estimates for this blueprint from the Heritage Auction Galleries were $60,000. That is valuable!

However, blueprints are valuable not just if they are written by Frank Lloyd Wright. Every blueprint is extremely valuable to the builders and owners. Why? If the engineer does a poor job, the integrity of the whole building is in jeopardy.

The same is true with a marriage. If God's blueprint is

not followed, then our whole marriage is on shaky ground –
or we could use Jesus' illustration, built on sand! Let's look
at God's blueprints for the roles of husband and wife in a
Christian marriage. We will begin with the believing
husband's role and then examine the believing wife's role.

The Believing Husband's Role

Let's now turn to the role of the husband as the head of the
family. Let's begin with the section in Ephesians regarding
husbands.

> "Husbands, love your wives, just as Christ also loved the
> church and gave Himself up for her, so that He might
> sanctify her, having cleansed her by the washing of water
> with the word, that He might present to Himself the
> church in all her glory, having no spot or wrinkle or any
> such thing; but that she would be holy and blameless. So
> husbands ought also to love their own wives as their own
> bodies. He who loves his own wife loves himself; for no
> one ever hated his own flesh, but nourishes and cherishes
> it, just as Christ also does the church, because we are
> members of His body. FOR THIS REASON A MAN
> SHALL LEAVE HIS FATHER AND MOTHER AND
> SHALL BE JOINED TO HIS WIFE, AND THE TWO
> SHALL BECOME ONE FLESH. *[Note: these capital letters
> indicate a quote from the Old Testament, in this case, the
> account from Genesis 2.]* This mystery is great; but I am
> speaking with reference to Christ and the church.
> Nevertheless, each individual among you also is to love his
> own wife even as himself, and the wife must *see to it* that
> she respects her husband" (Ephesians 5:25-33).

The Husband's Primary Obligation

"So husbands ought also to love their own wives as their own bodies. He who loves his own wife loves himself" (Ephesians 5:28).

Men, our high obligation is expressed in a four letter word called love. As we have learned in previous chapters, this is our highest goal. Love is the selfless service of another with no thought of return. We really get the most difficult of the roles in marriage.

Although we are all required to love one another, look at the extent of our love in this passage. That is where the mission impossible kicks in.

"Husbands, love your wives, just as Christ also loved the church and gave Himself up for her."

The *extent* of our love for our wives is as much as Christ loved the church. Also, we learn from this verse the highest *expression* of love ever shown – that of Jesus giving His life on the cross. His love was demonstrated in His giving His life. Christ's love for the church is an amazing thing! And that is our goal. That is what we are to emulate. That is the standard for whether or not we are loving enough. You must die for your wife.

For most of us, dying for our wives does not mean stepping in front of a bullet for them. Instead it requires a type of daily dying that may be more difficult than taking a bullet. You must daily give of yourself, your desires, and your aspirations until you are so worn out that you have no

more strength. This is daily dying for our wives and families. In one sense, when we become a husband, we no longer
have our own life. Our life is to die for our wives.

The Obligation Illustrated

If you are married, then you and your wife are one
person. You should treat your wife as you would yourself.
Now, the amount of time you spend in front of the mirror
may not be a good goal for you to use in giving yourself to
her. It may have been several weeks since you last looked in
the mirror. Nevertheless, this is a good illustration. Your
natural inclination is to protect yourself, to feed yourself, to
take care of all your basic needs. Helping, caring, and
sustaining are the natural responses of a person to their
body. When someone throws something at you as a surprise
(even if it is a small pillow), you automatically recoil. You put
your hands up in self-defense – we are made this way. This
is how a husband should treat his wife. It should be his
natural disposition to protect and care for his wife.

The Obligation Detailed

> "...for no one ever hated his own flesh, but nourishes and
> cherishes it, just as Christ also does the church"
> (Ephesians 5:29)

Don't hate your wife
Hate is a strong word. The sense is that this hatred is an
unthinkable thing for a husband to do toward his wife – no
one ever would do this! The reasoning of the text is that just
as no one would ever mistreat his own body (unless he was

out of his mind), no one would ever mistreat his wife. If you put your hand over a candle and hold your skin to the fire, we would wonder about your sanity. If someone mistreats his wife, we should likewise wonder about his sanity.

Hating should be out of the question in a Christian home. Unfortunately, the simple fact remains that it does happen. Men often mistreat their spouses to the point where their actions are the opposite of love. Love is unselfishly giving toward the other's well-being. The opposite is selfishly taking for your own well-being. Husbands would have to honestly acknowledge that this describes their behavior at times. Let it not be true!

Men, do you hate your wife? What is the tone you use with your voice when speaking with her? Do you put her desires and needs first or your own? Do you treat her in selfishness or in honor? This is a real question. Some folks can be nice to everyone else except their spouse. They will be congenial and sweet to ladies on the sidewalk or in line at the grocery store, but they treat their spouse like dirt. Be especially careful how you speak about your wife in public or in private. Remember the three following principles that we covered in an early lesson:

Be Careful What You Say – Her view of herself comes to a great extent from her best friend (that's you). Lift her up. Congratulate her.

Be Careful How You Say What You Say – The tone of our speech registers very deeply with our wives. Be careful to speak gently and graciously to your wife.

Be Careful Where You Say What You Say – Don't offer criticism or negative information in public. This should always be done behind closed doors. A husband should be always coming to the support of his wife in public, lifting her up.

After Paul handles the negative commands, he covers the positives.

Nourish and Cherish Her

Nourish – This is the word nurture. It harkens back to Christ's primary role to His bride, the church. He wants to sanctify, build, and grow her. Men, one of the primary roles of leadership is that by God's grace you would be involved in building your wife up in the faith. You must commit to helping her grow in the Word. What a value this would be to a church if every husband was concerned for his wife's and children's spiritual growth.

It is sad that often ladies are more attuned to spiritual things than men. It should not be this way. Just because this happens frequently does not mean that it is biblical.

Men must strive by God's grace to be strong spiritual leaders in their homes and in their sphere of influence.

The ideal church is where the pastor is helping husbands to disciple and build up their wives and children so that strong families are committed to Christ and following the Bible. This type of family changes a church and a city.

So, husbands, are you building up your family spiritually? Let me encourage you to begin by leading a brief Bible time with your family either every day or several times a week. These don't need to be profound teaching times, but simply reading God's Word or other age-appropriate Bible material to influence your children for Christ. This is a helpful way to put spiritual matters front and center. Even if you take five minutes to pray and read a section of Scripture, this demonstrates your desire to lead the family in this arena and will go a long way toward your wife and children making this an important part of their individual lives as well.

Cherish – The second word here is to cherish, *to warm, to keep warm, to cherish* with tender love, *to foster* with tender care. This has reference to gently taking care of someone or something. There is no bullying or belittling involved here. This is treating with respect and dignity. This is opening the door. This is handling with care in our speech and demeanor.

There is another passage that expands on this – let's look at it a bit here because it is the other passage in Scripture that gives lengthy instruction to husbands.

"You husbands in the same way, live with *your wives* in an understanding way, as with someone weaker, since she is a woman; and show her honor as a fellow heir of the grace of life, so that your prayers will not be hindered" (1 Peter 3:7).

Men, live with your wife in an understanding way. Understand them and how to love them. This is a life-long process. Learn what is best for them, understanding that she is a weaker vessel.

It is true that a woman is built differently than a man. We all realize that. Because of this, men are to treat women in a different way. You are to act as if she is a weaker vessel; she is like a valuable vase that we honor and set aside as special. Remember the Tiffany vase that we set out of the way of clumsy elbows and children's toys. This is the way we show honor. We set her aside and protect her from pain, from abuse, and from difficulty. Our life should be devoted to protecting and nurturing our wife.

Now I readily admit that although I might be stronger than Sarah I am probably not as tough. I think she has a higher tolerance for pain than I do. If you knew how I react to colds or discomforts, you would have to agree. So it is not who has a higher threshold for pain or saying that this lady is going to crumble if you say you don't like how she painted her nails. That is not the point. The point is no matter how tough or fragile your wife is physically or emotionally you should treat her as gently as possible. You honor her – you treat her with respect and kindness.

The Obligation Defended

"FOR THIS REASON A MAN SHALL LEAVE HIS FATHER AND MOTHER AND SHALL BE JOINED TO HIS WIFE, AND THE TWO SHALL BECOME ONE FLESH" (Ephesians 5:31).

Paul is Bible-driven. He quotes Scripture as the basis for his practice. Here Paul is quoting Genesis 2:24 (and thus the reason for the capital letters in this verse). There are three responsibilities given to the husband, though all three of them are really used to pinpoint what Paul has been emphasizing.

A husband should leave father and mother, be glued to his wife, and become one entity. You become members one of another. You are both one person now. There are not two identities; you are now one flesh. So it is painful to pry you apart. You could not be pried apart without organic and serious damage being done. That is what this entire passage has been about. "Treat your wife like you treat your own body." You can't be severed from your wife in any good fashion just as any head cannot be severed from a body in good fashion. That just doesn't work. You are together as one now.

Fulfilling Your Leadership Role

The Importance of Leadership

> "Wives, *be subject* to your own husbands, as to the Lord.
> For the husband is the head of the wife, as Christ also is
> the head of the church" (Ephesians 5:22-23).

We will look more carefully at these verses in the next
section, but it is clear from them that in God's blueprint for
the family, the husband is the head of the family unit. The
husband is to provide loving leadership for his wife and
children. Men, this is not something we can opt out of if we
are not spiritually mature enough or have had a difficult
week. We must obey this command.

Popular culture in our society cannot accept that a dad
should be the loving head of the home. They hate it.
However, that does not mean that we can rewrite God's
blueprint for the family for our day. These are the Words of
God; they stand while societies and other organizations rise
and fall. Let me point out the danger of throwing out this
role differential in a family. What does the role pattern? It
patterns Christ and the church. In other passages, it
patterns God the Father's role as well. We must realize that
God's ideal for the church, the Son, and the Father was
hashed out before there was a human alive on the earth. So
marriage is but a mirror of a deeper spiritual reality. When
we mar the mirror we mar the picture of Christ and the
church that God wants to show the world. So let us be
careful not to change God's blueprint. There are deeper
things going on here than our conflicts in the home. A

Gospel picture hangs in the balance. Let us take our role in that picture very seriously.

As a husband, perhaps you feel way out of your league when considering these duties. I agree with you whole-heartedly, but the Lord gives us the key to the type of leader He wants in the home. Let's look at the key to being a Godly leader in the home.

The Key to Leadership

How can we be a loving leader in our home? Jesus is the example in Ephesians 5, so we should go first to Him and consider how He was a leader. Let's look at Jesus' instruction on the key to leadership.

> "And there arose also a dispute among them as to which one of them was regarded to be greatest. And He said to them, 'The kings of the Gentiles lord it over them; and those who have authority over them are called "Benefactors." But it is not this way with you, but the one who is the greatest among you must become like the youngest, and the leader like the servant. For who is greater, the one who reclines at the table or the one who serves? Is it not the one who reclines at the table? But I am among you as the one who serves'" (Luke 22:24-27).

Others will follow in the footsteps of those who have washed their feet.
You cannot lead well those whom you have not served.

The disciples argued about who would take the highest leadership positions in the kingdom of God. Jesus taught that the leader is the one who serves. He later illustrated that as He took the place of the servant and washed their feet... then died for them. The secret to leading your family is washing their feet.

If you will be careful to lovingly serve your family; if you will take your desires, interests, and goals and place them on the back burner; if you will replace your desires with those of your family; if you will delight to help, care for, and serve your family, you will certainly find a family that delights to follow you.

I know that the problem with most men not being able to lead their families is that they have not been serving them. Dad's job does not mean just going to work to help pay the bills. This means coming home to listen, wash, work, and tirelessly spend yourself for your family. Your work does not end when you check out. Your most important work starts when you get home to your family. That is when you must serve the most. The home is not the man's castle where he is king. That is a horrible image of a man. The home is a palace where everyone is served, and the husband is the servant.

"But Tim," you object, "I can't do that! Are you kidding me?" Then you should have never gotten married. This is your role. A family is hard work, and you have no way of leading if you are not ready to serve. I like Pastor Paul Washer's response to this attitude: "Tough! You should have just gotten guinea pigs or something." I agree. If you are not ready to serve, you are not ready to be a husband. Can I say that this has been one of the worst things I have seen men do in their homes? Even pastors' homes become tyrannies if their only leadership is telling people what to do and reading a verse or two. That is horrible leadership. You are not leading if you are not serving. If we serve well, it will be a delight for our family to submit and to follow. They are just letting us serve them.

The Believing Wife's Role

Now that we have looked a little deeper into the context, let's focus on the passage that details the wife's role.

The Statement of the Command (5:22)

"Wives, *be subject* to your own husbands, as to the Lord."

The Action

The command here is simply stated – Wives be subject to your own husbands as to the Lord. There it is in black and white. The verb is in italics so it is good to understand again what is going on here. The verb is picked up from the previous verse. "Be subject one to another." Wives – be subject to your husbands. This verb is used 37 times in the New Testament and is used in many different relationships of submission. It is referring to arranging under the authority of another. The English form of the verb is made up of two different Greek concepts – one is the prefix "under," the other is "to arrange or order."

This is not the only time this principle occurs in Scripture. Let's look at a few other verses:

"Wives, be subject to your husbands, as is fitting in the Lord" (Colossians 3:18).

"A woman must quietly receive instruction with entire

submissiveness. [12] But I do not allow a woman to teach or exercise authority over a man" (1 Timothy 2:11-12).

"Older women . . . encourage the young women to love their husbands, to love their children, [5] to be sensible, pure, workers at home, kind, being subject to their own husbands, so that the word of God will not be dishonored" (Titus 2:3-5).

"In the same way, you wives, be submissive to your own husbands so that even if any of them are disobedient to the word, they may be won without a word by the behavior of their wives" (1 Peter 3:1).

Two Clarifications

1. This does not designate who is the most important in the marriage.

God is not referring to preference, giftedness, or class. This is not stating that the husband is a higher class or preferred above the women. No, before God we are all equal and are all accepted through Jesus (this is the message of Galatians 3:28). We are all made in the image of God, and if you look carefully at Genesis 1, we were both given the mandate to rule creation together – man and woman. The passage is not teaching that men are better than women. No, Paul is saying that in the home – in the family relationship – God has set an order. God desires order; and in His family order, there is a head of the family, the father.

Again, this is not saying that women are less important, less loved, or less valued than men. Even in the Trinity there is submission between perfectly equal Persons of the Godhead. In fact, when Jesus was on earth, He was in submission to His earthly parents. Listen to what Luke says about Jesus.

> "And He went down with them and came to Nazareth, and He continued in subjection to them; and His mother treasured all these things in her heart" (Luke 2:51).

Did you catch that? In the realm of the family, Jesus – Ruler of all Kings and Princes of all time, Creator of all that is, Sustainer of all that is – submitted Himself to His earthly mom and dad. He was not less important, but in the family He submitted Himself to His parents.

The wife's role is to arrange herself under her husband's headship. Of course, a loving husband will serve the family in his leadership role, but her posture will determine how much he can serve as a leader.

2. This does not designate who is the most gifted.

A second clarification: this is not stating who is the most gifted. You might say, "But my husband is lousy!" I'll respond – well, you married him. We realize, that in many relationships if you were to examine the wife's and the husband's IQs, hers might just double his. Or if you look at her gifts and people skills, you may think, "Wow she is loaded!... and he is just not quite there." I feel that way in my marriage. So the role of headship is not tied to giftedness but position.

A quick aside to husbands: as a leader you need to be smart enough to know your wife's abilities. If she is a skilled accountant and you are not, then you might need to ask her to balance the checkbook.

The Object Involved: To Your Own Husbands

I don't know that I really need to expand on this, but since it is here, I need to bring it out. Wives this is not a

submission to all the men in the world; it is to one individual, your own husband. This is not saying that women
always need to be subservient to men.

If we had a woman president, then as a citizen, I would
be subject to her in that sphere of life. In the family the wife
is subject to the husband. In government I am subject to the
governor with relationship to the rules of the land having to
do with citizenship (the one exception would be certain
aspects of church life; see 1 Timothy 2:11 above).

The Reason for the Command (5:23)

> "For the husband is the head of the wife, as Christ also is
> the head of the church, He Himself *being* the Savior of the
> body."

The reason is given in the illustration of a body. As the
head and the body are one, so the husband and wife are
one. They move together. The body responds to the leadership of the head, and this is done as a picture of the church's
response to Christ as the head. As a Christian lives out his or
her role in marriage, they picture Christ's relationship with
the church.

John Macarthur expands on this in his commentary on
Ephesians.

> "The head gives direction and the body responds. A
> physical body that does not respond to the direction of the
> head is crippled, or paralyzed. Likewise, a wife who does
> not properly respond to the direction of her husband
> manifests a serious spiritual dysfunction. On the other
> hand, a wife who willingly and lovingly responds to her
> husband's leadership as to the Lord is an honor to her

Lord, her husband, her family, her church, and herself. She is also a beautiful testimony to the Lord in view of the world around her."[1]

The wife is able to mirror the relationship that the church has to Jesus. This also gives the extent to which a wife is subject to her husband – in everything. Nancy Leigh DeMoss teaches this in her book *Lies Women Believe*.

> "When we place ourselves under the spiritual covering of the authorities God has placed in our lives, God protects us. On the other hand, when we insist on having it our way and stepping out from under that covering and protection, we open ourselves up to the influence and attack of the Enemy. I believe the failure of many Christian wives to place themselves under their husbands' authority accounts for the extent to which so many women are vulnerable to Satan's attack on their minds, wills, and emotions. When we come out from under authority – whether in big matters or seemingly insignificant areas – we become 'fair game' for the Enemy."[2]

Family Roles in Practice

Take an example of eating at Burger King or Taco Bell. If both agree on where to eat, there is no problem. Trouble comes, though, when the husband and wife disagree. That is where the  rubber meets the road, where the sinful nature comes in. The selfish wife wants to usurp the husband's headship: "Oh come on that place is gross!" The natural sinful response of the husband is to rule over her – it is to not even take into account her desires but to just overpower her and go wherever he wants. When there is a disagreement there should be these three steps:

The first step is communication:

Each person gives his or her view. She loves the little toys that they are giving in the kid's meals. While the husband may say, "But I love the taste of the beefless beef that they serve at Taco Bell."

There are rules that should govern their communication. You notice that I said *communication* not *argumentation*. The difference between communicating your reasons and arguing your position depends much upon your spirit and manner in giving the communication:

- Loving (in tone, manner, controlled),
- Open ("Well I don't really care..." – no share),
- Truthful (Taco Bell meat is the most nutritious.)

You can accomplish a L.O.T. if you keep those rules in mind – Loving, Open, Truthful.

The second step is decision:

It is the husband's role to make the decision – he incorporates this new knowledge, and then he makes the decision. The loving spirit-filled husband will respond in love to his family and set aside his desires for what is best for the family. And the wife will say, "What are you doing? I thought you wanted to go to Taco Bell – no! Let's go to Taco Bell instead . . . it's not really a big deal to me."

Here you have the husband pleasing his wife, and the wife pleasing her husband and you have that locomotive working well . . . the engine's pistons firing back and forth and back and forth.

The third step is response:

Once the decision is made then the wife should get behind her husband and support him. We don't get into Taco Bell, and the wife says – "Oh, I don't really want anything anyway." You know how it happens. "This was your decision . . . but I'm going to make you hate your decision and show you repeatedly how wrong it was for you to choose this!"

Three simple steps: Communication, decision, and response. Three simple steps. This process was easy when talking about a meal at night. However, those steps will be more difficult and more time consuming when it is something like employment, education, and finances.

Chapter 8 Homework

1. Husbands, what is your primary role toward your wife?

2. What are ways that husbands "hate" their wives?

3. Men, are you providing spiritual leadership for your wife? If not, what are some ways you can take serious steps toward leading her?

4. What is Jesus' key to Christian leadership in the home?

5. All Christians are commanded to submit to one another in our relationships (True / False).

6. Submission refers to inferiority (True / False).

9

DEVELOPING A SATISFYING
RELATIONSHIP

Loving

Biblical Principles for Developing
& Maintaining Loving Relationships

W
hat a joy great relationships are in life! I trust
that the biblical principles from these pages
have been a very practical way for you to
build and maintain strong relationships in your own life. I
especially pray that your marriage will be much stronger
and more stable for it. I would like to leave you with one
very important and overarching thought; only one relationship can satisfy you.

Sadly, people often try to find satisfaction in their relationships when we know that is not possible. Only God can
fill the satisfying role in our lives, and if we try to make a
relationship with a spouse, friend, or child take the place of
the role God should play in our lives, we have actually just
made an idol.

I often hear counselors, even Christian counselors, give
advice that goes along these lines: "You need to adjust this
behavior and continue that habit in marriage so that you
can make your spouse happy." Or, "Men have this need and
women have this need." Our job is to meet that need so they
are happy. I realize that we are all different, but in all this

counsel, and even in the principles written in this booklet, if we are not careful we are setting up human relationships as an end in themselves. If you finally get him or her to do this then you will be happy! Whereas, we must remember that only one relationship will truly meet the need of humanity.

If I rely on a right relationship with a spouse to satisfy me then I am holding that relationship in an improper way. I receive joy and I glorify God in my relationship with my spouse, but I will never have ultimate satisfaction or ultimate fulfillment in family or any other human relationship outside of my relationship with God.

Perhaps we set marriages up for failure if we set the picture of the family, children, and white picket fence as that which will satisfy or bring joy. Only Christ can bring that satisfaction.

Jesus gave the woman at the well this instruction. He used the illustration of thirst/quenching thirst with water. She had relationships with many different men seeking to find satisfaction in them. She thought that the thirst of her soul could be satisfied in human relationships, but that is not the case. Jesus encouraged her to believe in Him and that the relationship with Him would cause her to have a never-ending flow of water springing up from inside of her. As a result, her thirst would always be quenched even without any spouse.

> "Jesus answered and said to her, 'Everyone who drinks of this water will thirst again; but whoever drinks of the water that I will give him shall never thirst; but the water that I will give him will become in him a well of water springing up to eternal life'" (John 4:13-14).

Having right relationships on earth is very important.

But it does not quench the thirst of the heart that can only be quenched with a right relationship with the God of heaven through Jesus Christ.

Matthew Henry emphasizes this in one of my favorite devotional books *The Pleasantness of a Religious Life.*[1]

> "I have found that satisfaction in communion with God, which I would not exchange for all the delights of the sons of men, and the peculiar treasures of kings and provinces." (pg. 98)

> "Here is bait that has no hook under it, a pleasure courting you which has no pain attending it, no bitterness at the latter end of it; a pleasure which God himself invites you to, and which will make you happy, truly and eternally happy." (pg. 45).

Setting up a romantic view of the perfect marriage or any other relationship can quickly become idolatrous. Only Christ is our soul's true satisfaction. If we try to find in a spouse what we can find only in our God, then we are committing idolatry.

But we can find a joyful gift from our loving heavenly Father in these earthly relationships. We find in them the grace to worship Him more as we build one another closer to Him. We find in our marriages the privilege of displaying to all Christ's relationship with the church. If we keep this in perspective, then we will have fulfilled our goal as fellow travelers on the road of life. At the end of the road, in heaven itself, the relationships never end but are enjoyed without sin, tears, or sorrow. That will truly be a glorious family reunion!

O Christ, He is the fountain,
The deep, sweet well of love!
The streams of earth I've tasted
More deep I'll drink above:
There to an ocean fullness
His mercy doth expand,
And glory, glory dwelleth
In Immanuel's land.[2]

10

ANNUAL CHECKUP: ARE YOU A LOVING PERSON?

Loving

Biblical Principles for Developing
& Maintaining Loving Relationships

L et's answer that question objectively. This appendix is designed to apply the actions of love to our lives in a practical way. Ideally, every person should go through this check-up once a year. There is space to develop each activity of love.

Step 1 – Go through each of the 15 activities of love and detail areas where you are weak in a particular activity (try to include at least two). Then write areas you see that you could develop positively in the future in that specific activity. The first activity of patience is done to illustrate how to fill out the entire exercise.

Step 2 – Once you have filled the exercise out for yourself, take time to answer the questions for your spouse. Indicate ways he or she can improve in each area. Limit yourself to two examples for any one action of love, and be sure to exercise the rules of biblical communication!

Step 3 – Once you are both done, set down a time where you can both sit down and review the discoveries one with another. This is a way for us to constantly improve our relationships. We never stop building! If you are able, try to make this event a fun event such as a bed and breakfast outing over a Friday and Saturday.

Be specific. We are tempted to speak only in generalities. Giving specific examples will give our spouses concrete ways to improve in the future. The following is an example of how you might use this to detail areas of needed improvement.

1. Love is patient – A loving person will endure a lot of "heat" before they "boil."

Ways you have failed to love this way in the past:	*Ways you can demonstrate love with this action in the future:*
I have failed to be patient with how much time you want to spend speaking with your mom and dad on the phone.	Provide you with helpful time with your parents, while I watch the children.
On the weekends, I get stressed out with the noise that comes from our children and I am quick to tell everyone to stop talking.	Take a quick stroll while the kiddos get loud and then come back in five minutes more ready to be exuberant with the rest of the family.
I get tired of your telling me we can't buy certain things.	Plan out the way to purchase things and not be impatient with not having money now.

1. Love is patient – A loving person will endure a lot of "heat" before they "boil."

Self-Evaluation:

Ways you have failed to be patient in the past:	Ways you can demonstrate patience in the future:

Constructive suggestions for my spouse:

...failed to be patient in the past:	Ways to demonstrate patience in the future:

2. Love is kind – Kindness is treating others as you
   would like to be treated; to be easy with
   someone.

Self-Evaluation:

Ways you have failed to be kind in the past:	*Ways you can demonstrate kindness in the future:*

Constructive suggestions for my spouse:

...failed to be kind in the past:	*Ways to demonstrate kindness in the future:*

3. Love is not jealous – Love is not jealous of the positive things that happen to another, but rejoices.

Self-Evaluation:

Ways you were jealous in the past:	Ways you can rejoice in your spouse's success:

Constructive suggestions for my spouse:

...jealous in the past:	...ways to rejoice in the positive in the future:

4. Love does not brag – Love does not focus on self-promotion in conversation.

Self-Evaluation:

Ways you were braggadocios in the past:	Ways you can talk positively of others:

Constructive suggestions for my spouse:

Ways he or she was braggadocios in the past:	Ways he or she can talk positively of others:

5. Love is not arrogant – Love is not puffed up. It does not have an exaggerated view of self.

Self-Evaluation:

Ways you were arrogant in the past:	Ways you can walk in humility in the future:

Constructive suggestions for my spouse:

Ways he or she was arrogant in the past:	Ways he or she can walk in humility in the future:

6. Love is not rude – Love does not act in a way that is unbecoming or improper for the setting.

Self-Evaluation:

Ways you were rude in the past:	Ways you can be more considerate in the future:

Constructive suggestions for my spouse:

Ways he or she was rude in the past:	Ways he or she can be more considerate:

7. Love does not seek its own – Love is not solely concerned about one's own ideas and goals. It is not selfish.

Self-Evaluation:

Ways you were self-consumed in the past:	Ways you can be interested in your spouse in the future:

Constructive suggestions for my spouse:

Ways he or she was self-consumed in the past:	Ways he or she can be interested in you in the future:

8. Love is not easily provoked – It does not easily fly of the handle, but is slow to retaliate.

Self-Evaluation:

Ways you were easily provoked in the past:	Ways you can be more patient in the future:

Constructive suggestions for my spouse:

Ways he or she was easily provoked in the past:	Ways he or she can be more patient in the future:

9. Love does not take into account a wrong suffered – Love does not hold grudges.

Self-Evaluation:

Times you held a grudge in the past:	*Ways you can be more forgiving in the future:*

Constructive suggestions for my spouse:

Times he or she held a grudge in the past:	*Ways he or she can be more forgiving in the future:*

10. Love does not rejoice in unrighteousness but rejoices in the truth – Love tries to think the best about situations and about their spouse. It is a "cheer leader" for their spouse.

Self-Evaluation:

Times you did not rejoice with your spouse:	Ways you can be enthusiastic in the future:

Constructive suggestions for my spouse:

Times he or she did not rejoice with your spouse:	Ways he can be more enthusiastic in the future:

11. Love bears (covers) all things - Love protects and
    tries to cover the fault of the other spouse.

Self-Evaluation:

Times you failed to protect or cover your spouse's faults:	Ways you can better protect your spouse:

Constructive suggestions for my spouse:

Times he or she failed to protect or cover your faults:	Ways he or she can better protect you or cover for your faults:

12/13. Love believes/hopes all things – Love trusts the other spouse. Also, consider ways you can develop trustworthiness.

Self-Evaluation:

Times you did think the best were untrusting:	Ways you can be more trusting in the future:

Constructive suggestions for my spouse:

Times you did think the best were untrusting:	Ways you can be more trusting in the future:

14. Love endures all things – Love bears up under the pressure arising from being with your spouse.

Self-Evaluation:

Times you did endure well in the past:	Ways you can endure all things with your spouse in the future:

Constructive suggestions for my spouse:

Times you did endure well in the past:	Ways you can endure all things with your spouse in the future:

15. Love never fails – Love is always consistent and reliable in acting toward the other's wellbeing.

Self-Evaluation:

Times or areas you have failed to love in the past:	*Ways you can be more reliable in your love in the future:*

Constructive suggestions for my spouse:

Times or areas you have failed to love in the past:	*Ways you can be more reliable in your love in the future:*

NOTES

1. Love Defined

1. I remember one marriage counselor encouraging the counselees to treat their loving activities as a bank account. As they did something loving to their spouse, they deposited into the relationship bank. They were encouraged to continue to deposit enough so there would be enough there to withdraw at a future time. As they needed things in the future from that relationship there would be enough to withdraw. That is horrible advice! That is not love. I am so thankful that the Lord does not treat us this way. Love continues to deposit 100% even if the other spouse deposits nothing. If that is too hard for you to consider, then you will need God's help to redefine love. You have covenanted before God and witnesses to love in sickness and health, for better or for worse, not just when the other person deposited enough into your love bank.
2. "But God demonstrates His own love toward us, in that while we were yet sinners, Christ died for us" (Romans 5:8).

2. Love Described Part 1

1. Unlike most English translations, which include several adjectives, the Greek forms of all those properties are verbs. They do not focus on what love is so much as on what love does and does not do (John MacArthur, *Commentary on 1 Corinthians*; Chicago: Moody, 1984. Page 337).
2. From *Charity and Its Fruits*, Chapter 6 – "Charity inconsistent with an envious spirit"
3. R. A. Torrey *Why God Used D. L. Moody* (Create Space Independent Publishing Platform, 2016).
4. Ibid.
5. "'I suppose you are quite a great lawyer?' I said, after looking at him for some time.

    'Me, Master Copperfield?' said Uriah. 'Oh, no! I'm a very umble person.'... 'I am well aware that I am the umblest person going,' said Uriah Heep, modestly; 'let the other be where he may. My mother is likewise a very umble person. We live in an umble abode, Master Copperfield, but have much to be thankful for.'"

3. Love Described Part 2

1. I'll make a quick application to pastors' speech from the pulpit. For some being crass or uncouth has become a common "attention getter." This is not love. Love puts off rude speech. Martin Lloyd-Jones dealt with the same thing sixty years ago. Lloyd-Jones mentions a chaplain that was known to become like his soldiers to reach them. He took to smoking and cursing to attract other men.

   "After the end of the Second World War he used to go around the country teaching this and urging that preachers must do this; and many tried to do so and began to do so. But the verdict of history on this was that it was a complete failure, a temporary 'stunt' or 'gimmick' that achieved notoriety for a while but soon entirely disappeared from thinking of the church. From the standpoint of the New Testament it was based on a complete fallacy. Our Lord attracted sinners because He was different... This idea that our going to win people to the Christian faith by showing that after all you are remarkably like them, is theologically and psychologically a profound blunder." From "Preaching and Preachers" by Martyn Lloyd-Jones, Harper and Collins, Pg. 139.
2. Amityville, NY: Calvary Press, 1999.

5. Communicating in Love

1. This is the concept in George Eliot's *Daniel Deronda*. Gwendolen, the beautiful young lady who is now devoid of independent wealth, thinks of trying to earn her way in the world through her voice. So, she goes to the world-renowned musician Klesmer to see if he thinks she has enough ability to support herself in theater. She too gets the unvarnished truth from him: "Measuring probabilities, my judgment is... You will hardly achieve more than mediocrity." This was not what she wanted to hear, nor was it said in a tone she wanted to hear.
2. *Ephesians*, p. 201
3. John and Elizabeth Sherrill, *God's Smuggler*. Several editions, chapter 5.

6. Forgiving in Love

1. Jo's experience has been recorded in the book *Journey to Murder: Road to Forgiveness*.

7. Fulfilling Your Role in Love Part 1

1. Teng Leng Ooi; quoted in Cell Press, "Push and pull get eyes to work together." *ScienceDaily*, 17 October 2010.

8. Fulfilling Your Role in Love Part 2

1. Chicago: Moody Publishers, 1986. Pages 288-289.
2. Chicago: Moody Publishers, 2002. Pages 148-149.

9. Developing a Satisfying Relationship

1. The Pleasantness of a Religious Life: Life as good as it can be. Christian Focus Publications edition, 2012.
2. From Anne Cousin's Hymn, "The Sands of Time Are Sinking"

Made in the USA
Columbia, SC
15 July 2024